Commend

The Anointing: Yesterday, Today, Tomorrow

'An important message for the Church today is wrapped in an immensely readable and compelling mixture; moving personal glimpses into R T's life from early years in Kentucky to the pulpit in Westminster Chapel today are combined with theological insights and very helpful, practical teaching for Christians of all ages. R T is a no-label man of God breathing his message of word and Spirit in every chapter – fascinating and inspiring.'

Rev Sandy Millar
Vicar, Holy Trinity Brompton

'R T is a man of complete integrity and deserves to be heard. When one personally knows that the author is a man of prayer with a deep longing for more of God, then you want to read what he has to say.'

Rev Robert Amess
Senior Minister, Duke Street Baptist Church, Richmond

'I could not put this book down. If every Christian read it and took notice of its contents, God alone knows what might happen amongst us.'

Rev Lyndon Bowring
Executive Chairman, CARE

'All of us have moments in our life and ministry when God activates the rudder of his word to direct us. The inspiration of this book has been a formative influence in my own ministry. In *The Anointing: Yesterday, Today, Tomorrow* Dr Kendall gives us the benefit of his knowledge and the vulnerability of his own testimony, to steer us away from becoming yesterday's people, remaining in God's purposes today.'

Rev Joel Edwards
General Director, Evangelical Alliance

'A great book. Very readable. Very challenging. It should become a classic.'

Dr Michael Eaton
Nairobi, Kenya

'It is excellent. It is so fresh and quite unlike anything else available on the subject. It accurately portrays where the Church is today in regard to things of the Spirit. The book will make people hungry for more, while appreciating what God is doing today. R T (Dr Kendall) carries a rare, even unique, combination – respect for God's work in the past, sensitivity to what the Spirit is doing today and hunger for the greater things yet to come.'

Rev Colin Dye
Senior Minister, Kensington Temple

The Anointing

Yesterday, Today, Tomorrow

R T Kendall

Hodder & Stoughton

LONDON SYDNEY AUCKLAND

British Library Cataloguing in Publication Data
A record for this book is available from the British Library

ISBN 0 340 72144 8

Typeset by Avon Dataset Ltd, Bidford-on-Avon, Warks
Printed and bound in Great Britain by
Clays Ltd St Ives plc, Bungay, Suffolk

Hodder and Stoughton
A division of Hodder Headline PLC
338 Euston Road
London NW1 3BH

To T R

Contents

Preface

I follow a Bible reading plan that was designed by Robert Murray M'Cheyne. I was not prepared for what I received one morning when, in the normal course of my daily Bible reading, 1 Samuel 16:1 leaped out at me:

> The Lord said to Samuel, 'How long will you mourn for Saul, since I have rejected him as king over Israel? Fill your horn with oil and be on your way; I am sending you to Jesse of Bethlehem. I have chosen one of his sons to be king.'

In a flash I saw three eras: yesterday's man (King Saul), today's man (Samuel), tomorrow's man (David). That insight gave birth to this book.

As always, I am indebted to many people for help in writing my books. Special thanks to my editor, Annabel Robson, of Hodder & Stoughton. I thank her for her probing questions and patience.

My secretary, Sheila Penton, is one of the few people on earth who can decipher my handwriting! I thank her most warmly for her care and hard work.

A good number of friends have kindly read the manuscript. I want to thank Lyndon Bowring and Michael Eaton in particular for their helpful suggestions. I am honoured that Rob Parsons agreed to write a Foreword.

My first book with Hodder's was *Jonah* and I dedicated it to my wife Louise and our two children: Melissa Louise and Robert Tillman (whom, for some reason, we have always called 'T R'!). I was so sure that book would be my last that I made certain they were a part of it. But I have since wanted to dedicate a book to each of them at some stage. That time has begun to arrive.

I dedicate this book to our son T R. Being my son has not been easy for him. Paul Cain always said that T R needs to see 'life after life'. What Paul means by this is that in addition to the sound doctrine that T R has had all his life, he needed to discover for himself how real God is. This happened, and I tell a little of it in the pages that follow.

My deepest thanks as always go to my wife Louise for her love and encouragement.

R T Kendall
February 1998

Foreword

Sometimes, when I sit at home on a rainy Saturday morning, my mind goes to the heart of London. The picture is very clear. I can see a normally busy road that's quieter now on this weekend day. There's a hotel just along the street, and if I were to amble around a corner I would find myself at Scotland Yard. There are few people about but suddenly I see him. He is dressed in a black overcoat and wears a cap. As people approach him, he speaks with them and I can see he is giving out literature. I sometimes smile as I think of this eminent theologian and biblical scholar on the streets every Saturday morning sharing with whoever cares to listen the message of the risen Christ. And I smile because I admire him. There are many preachers, including me, who talk about evanglism, but he has a passion not just for what the Bible says about it, but for what God might just *do* about it.

And there's the key to the man. R T Kendall is dedicated to the search for the God of the Bible who acts *today*. Such a search is by, its very nature, dangerous. Theology is 'safe' as long as it is kept in the realm of discussion and imprisoned in the walls of academia. On the other hand, the world is full of those who want only to talk of their 'experiences' and have little time for a serious consideration of the Bible. The search has cost him dearly and in several ways. First and most predictably there are the critics. The interesting thing about R T Kendall is his ability to fall out with people at both ends of the theological spectrum. But far deeper than the barbs is the inner battle of desperately wanting to see a body of people rise up who have a high view of Scripture and a belief that the God who wrote it is still active today; in short, a yearning for the coming together of the Word and the Spirit.

I just happened to have been asked to read the manuscript of this book in my fiftieth year. I have found that half-century mark sobering. Life is short. As I read I found an ache developing in my heart that by God's grace I might not miss out on what the Spirit wants to do in this generation. It is not enough that we be theologically sound, nor sufficient to be seen to be successful, and it is certainly not enough to be busy. We need the anointing.

The nightmares we have tend to change as we get older. The bogey men of our childhood get replaced with far more terrifying spectres. I believe one of them is in this book. It is to be yesterday's man or woman and not know it – somebody who has lost the anointing of God on their lives but goes on as though nothing has changed. As R T Kendall paints that picture, we realise that only two people know what's happened to such a person: God himself and then the man or woman themselves who realise as the years go by that they are trying to live on yesterday's touch of God.

But the vision at the heart of this book is so different. It is of a body of people – most of them ordinary people – who crave that the God of the Bible be seen at work in our nation and our lives today. The majority of them will never hit the headlines but if Dr Kendall is right, they have the power to turn the world upside down, for in their hearts, and minds and spirits they can know the anointing of God himself.

I pray with all my heart that neither you nor I miss it.

Rob Parsons
February 1998

Introduction

There are two men who have had considerable influence on me since I have been at Westminster Chapel: Dr D Martyn Lloyd-Jones and Dr Paul Cain.

It may seem strange to mention these two men in the same sentence since they were in some ways poles apart theologically – and have come from opposite ends of the Church – but they have had one thing in common: an openness to the immediate and direct witness of the Holy Spirit.

Next to my father, Dr Lloyd-Jones has had more influence on me than anyone else. He put me where I am and taught me how to think. Dr Cain's experiences in the realm of healing and prophecy took me right back to my early years and gave me renewed confidence that what I myself had experienced need not be swept under the carpet. In an incredible manner the influence of these two men coalesced.

Dr Lloyd-Jones opened his door to me immediately after I came to Westminster Chapel. We had a standing date every Thursday – from eleven to one o'clock – when Mrs Lloyd-Jones would bring in coffee and KitKat biscuits. I read every word of my preparation for the three services the following weekend. For most of the first four years, virtually every word I uttered publicly in my pulpit had been heard first by him. Surely no minister this century had such a privilege as I. I could see how his mind worked. I asked him hundreds of questions. I shared with him my secrets and fears. He was like a father to me. I felt so much love from him.

One day in October 1990 I was invited to have lunch with a man I'd never met before. I decided I'd like to have a friend with me, and I phoned Lyndon Bowring.

'Are you free for lunch?' I asked.

'Well,' he said. 'It won't be easy.'

'I bet you are,' I interrupted.

'Who is it?' he asked.

'Paul Cain.'

'I'll be there,' Lyndon said at once.

My wife and I prayed together before I headed for Paul's hotel: 'Lord, don't let me be deceived if this man is a false prophet, but don't let me misjudge him if he is from you.'

The three of us ate lunch at the Tower Thistle Hotel overlooking the Thames. I came away four hours later feeling I had just met the brother I never had. In fact Paul said to me that the Lord showed him before we met that I would be the brother *he* never had.

Dr Lloyd-Jones's wisdom was invaluable. Although he tended to err on the side of caution, he would often say, 'Very well, you go on.' He was not a man who took many risks himself but he would often set me free to do and to preach what was burning on my heart. He loved, for example, my vision of 'Isaac', that for thirteen years Abraham sincerely believed that Ishmael was the promised son. But one day God said to Abraham, 'Wrong. Isaac is coming' (Gen. 17:15–21). In much the same way some sincere Christians have assumed that the charismatic movement is 'it' – the revival the Church has been praying for. Wrong. Isaac is coming. This means a movement of the Holy Spirit will be so vast and powerful, surpassing anything this century has seen, even in proportion to the promise and significance of Isaac when compared with Ishmael.

A few weeks after meeting Paul Cain I shared my conviction about Isaac, fearing that Paul would be offended. 'I have preached that for twenty years *to* charismatics,' said Paul. The more I spent time with Paul the more I was in awe of God's providence that I should meet and get to know such unusual men.

Dr Lloyd-Jones was primarily a Bible expositor, arguably the greatest in church history. No one has matched his genius. And yet his openness to the Holy Spirit was equal to his love for the word; it would be impossible to tell which was more important to him. His gift lay primarily with understanding the scriptures but he was fond of those who were open to the immediate and direct witness of the Spirit more than those who were merely 'sound'. Of the latter he would sometimes say, 'Perfectly orthodox, perfectly useless'.

Paul Cain's attraction to me was based on my adherence to the word. He felt deprived in his own knowledge of the Bible and good theology. He asked to be a member of Westminster Chapel. He has probably heard me preach more than anybody other than my own congregation. I have often cautioned him: 'Paul, do you realise what you are asking for – to be under my ministry? Don't you realise I am reformed in my theology? How do you know you are being led by God to us?' His reply: 'All my life I've sought to hear from God.' He assured me God brought him to us.

One Monday morning, 31 October 1955, driving from near Palmer, Tennessee, back to where I was a student at Trevecca Nazarene College of Nashville, the glory of the Lord filled my car. All of a sudden there was Jesus himself interceding before the Father on my behalf. I had never witnessed anything like it. I wept with joy as I drove. When I get to Heaven I want to see a video replay of the whole thing – if only to know how I was able to drive the next sixty miles. All I now remember was an hour later, coming past Smyrna, Tennessee, when I heard Jesus say to the Father, 'He wants it.' The Father answered back, 'He can have it.' In that moment the most incredible warmth and peace surged into my heart as if a liquid flame had entered. It was tangible. I beheld the face of Jesus for several seconds, less than a minute. The experience ended. Ten minutes later I got out of my car, went to my room and shaved, then went to my first class at Trevecca.

The experience changed my theology. I thought I had discovered something new, that I must have been the first since the Apostle Paul to have experienced and believed what I felt. In hours I was not only transformed but also reformed in my theology, but I didn't realise that then. It was a theology, however, which led me out of my old denomination (which I still love and respect) and eventually led me to England and my present church.

I told all the above to Dr Lloyd-Jones. If I am honest, it is what he loved most about me. But I tended to put the supernatural aspect of my experience to one side and believed the Lord called me to be faithful in expository preaching at Westminster Chapel. That has not changed to the present moment. My old experience, combined with the way Dr Lloyd-Jones taught me to think, kept me open to *anybody* in whom I saw an unusual anointing. And when God brought Paul Cain into my life I began to see that all I had experienced years ago was with a sovereign purpose that was beginning to make even more sense to me. The initial experience of 31 October 1955 was followed by a series of visions which would come to me over about a year. Some of them have been fulfilled, others remain unfulfilled.

When I first heard things about Paul Cain, I feared he was occultic. That was until I met him face to face. Months later I got to spend a lot of time with him and to observe how his gift functions. One evening he and I were relaxing in my home, when the phone rang. It was Benjamin Chan, one of our members (now a deacon), who asked if we'd like Chinese food the next day. Two years previously I had held little William Chan's warm body in my arms only moments after he died; the operation on the hole in his heart had failed. The parents had prayed for a sign that their two-year-old son was truly in Heaven. I assured them that he was safe in Jesus' arms but they still wanted more assurance. Since then they have been given another son, Wing Yung. Now Paul Cain knew *nothing* of this, nor had he met or heard of this godly couple. When I put the phone down Paul spoke up: 'William – hole in the heart, now in Heaven. That isn't a Chinese name, is it, but they now have a son – Wing Yung.' You can imagine Benjamin's astonishment and joy when I immediately phoned back what Paul had said.

My father, however, had the greatest influence on me. My earliest memories of him are of seeing him on his knees at his chair in our living room in Ashland, Kentucky. He was not a pracher, he was a clerk at the Chesapeake and Ohio Railway Company. He taught a Sunday School class in our church. Though a layman, he would not even think of going to work before spending thirty minutes alone with God. I have yet to meet a man I admired more. God has been singularly good to me to give me such a father. 'The boundary lines have fallen for me in pleasant places; surely I have a delightful inheritance,' said David (Ps. 16:6).

As we consider the anointing and ultimately the coming together of the word and the Spirit we will focus on three biblical characters: King Saul, whom I see as a type of yesterday's man (or anointing); the prophet Samuel, a symbol representing today's man; and David, an example of tomorrow's man. The book consequently is in three parts: Yesterday's Anointing, Today's Anointing, Tomorrow's Anointing. It is my belief that tomorrow's anointing will result in the long-awaited combination, prophesied by Smith-Wigglesworth in 1947, of the word and Spirit. I long for that day.

INTRODUCING THE ANOINTING

The Anointing

One of the most frightening comments I have heard since I entered the ministry was uttered by an Episcopalian priest in America: 'If the Holy Spirit were taken completely from the Church, 90 per cent of the work of the Church would go right on as if nothing had happened!'

What a travesty of what the Church was meant to be! And can it be true also of our personal lives – that many of us are churning out 'Christian' activity that has no touch of God upon it?

There is only one antidote to such a situation: it is breathtaking in its possibility, it is awesome in its power, it is liberating in its effect. It is quite simply – the anointing.

I will never forget an incident that occurred a few years ago. It was when I was with Jackie Pullinger. I had walked with her in the Walled City of Hong Kong and watched her minister to ex-drug addicts. I was scared at just being in that part of the city but Jackie had now lived there for twenty years. I was amazed at all God had achieved through this woman. Later on came an off-the-cuff comment: 'R T,' she said, 'To the spiritual person the supernatural seems natural.'

The anointing is the power of the Holy Spirit. At the end of the day there is no better definition. This book is about the power of the Holy Spirit. But there is a more refined definition which I would like to offer at this stage.

Several years ago someone came into my vestry and asked me, 'What do you mean by the anointing?' I remember replying something like this: 'It's a gift that functions easily when it's working.' I had never said it like that before but I must have thought it. The seed for this thought probably came from what Jackie Pullinger had said. The person who is filled with the Holy Spirit is able to do extraordinary things but to them it seems quite natural. It is easy. That is, when it's working.

It does not follow of course that *all* which functions easily is one's anointing. Some things come easily that are not necessarily good – eating, talking too much or watching more television than is good for one. Temptation comes easily and we may find it 'natural' to do things that are not productive. The anointing, however, leads to what is good; it blesses and encourages others. And its function is carried out with ease and without strain or fatigue. It is also self-edifying.

I say: when it is *working* it functions easily. The late John Wimber kindly called on me in my vestry a couple of years ago. While we were talking I heard Bill Reynolds' voice outside the door. Bill is our church secretary and one of our deacons. I thought he might like to meet John so I went to get him. As soon as I introduced him John began to prophesy to him: 'You're like Cornelius whose prayers have come up as a remembrance to God.' And then John prophesied about Bill's two sons. John had no way of knowing he had two sons, but what stunned Bill was that Paul Cain had said the same thing to him about those two sons three years before! I remarked, 'Well, Bill, I bet you didn't expect that when I called you in here!' Bill was staggered at this, whereupon John said in a matter-of-fact manner, 'I can't turn it on and I can't turn it off.'

When the anointing is working it is as natural and easy for our gift to function as eating or talking with friends. The gift is always there but doesn't always function easily. The anointing on that gift makes it function with ease. A further example of this was when I was doing the Bible readings at Spring Harvest in 1994. That year I preached at both Minehead and Skegness. When I preached through Isaiah 49 at Minehead I felt unusual help – there was a definite anointing on my preaching (at least I felt it). I assumed that when I repeated the same sermon a week later at Skegness I would have the same experience. Wrong. I struggled, preached with nervousness and thought it would never end! I couldn't believe the contrast between the two occasions although I had the same set of notes for each.

You can't turn it on and you can't turn it off. That *doesn't* mean one loses control when the anointing unexpectedly emerges. 'The spirits of prophets are subject to the control of prophets' (1 Cor. 14:32). But Jesus said, 'The wind blows wherever it pleases' (John 3:8), and one is continually surprised over the unexpected moment when the Holy Spirit flows from within.

The problem is, life goes on and we do our best with the gifts we have. One has to go to work whether one feels like it or not. I have to prepare three or four new sermons or lectures weekly whether I feel like it or not. I have to speak several times a week whether I feel like it or not. There are times when there is such an anointing on my preparation that I can hardly wait to preach. There are also times (most of the time, if I'm honest) when I work and work with no great feeling of inspiration. Once in a while my whole sermon preparation unfolds in seconds and the preaching of it is as good (or better) than when the preparation took days.

This is true no matter what one's calling is. A Spirit-filled nurse may be walking down a hospital corridor to give a patient an injection when she suddenly feels a sense of God's presence. She continues with her work but does so with the knowledge that God is with her in a special way. There is no greater feeling. Whether one is a secretary, professional person, homemaker, lorry driver or minister, the possibility of the anointing is there all the time; one never knows when God will manifest himself in an unusual way. Therefore, in my own work – whether in public speaking or in the solitude of intense preparation – I never know when that sense of God will come on me.

Why? There are probably *two* explanations. First, me. My mood, how much sleep I had, who I have just been talking with, how clear my mind feels, whether I am rushed or having to meet a deadline. It could be largely physical or emotional. It has much to do with whether I am under pressure. Or even if I have something to look forward to, like spending time with a trusted friend. It may therefore have little to do with the Holy Spirit. The second explanation is the sovereignty of the person of the Holy Spirit. The anointing *is* the Holy Spirit and the Holy Spirit is a person. God the Father is a person with a personality. God the Son – Jesus Christ – is a person with a personality. The Holy Spirit likewise has his own personality. He therefore moves in at will when we least expect it, and sometimes when we are least deserving of it. A lot of prayer no doubt has something to do with it, but there are times when the Spirit operates sovereignly when I haven't prayed as much as I should. The anointing is unmerited favour – it is sheer grace.

'Gift' and 'anointing' are words that can sometimes be used interchangeably but the liveliness of the anointing determines whether that gift works at its best. One should pray for the anointing on one's gift – or even pray for an anointing on one's anointing! This is because of the various ways the Holy Spirit manifests himself. Whereas he is on deposit in every Christian (Rom. 8:9; 1 Cor. 12:11-13), he can be grieved (Eph. 4:30) or quenched (1 Thess. 5:19). He is said to have '*departed*' from Saul (1 Sam. 16:14) and yet the Spirit came on him *after that* and he prophesied (1 Sam. 19:23)! Saul was rejected as king (1 Sam. 16:1) but was still referred to as anointed (1 Sam. 24:6). This is why 'gift' and 'anointing' can be used in much the same way and yet the term 'anointing' is used in more than one way.

The anointing functioning at its best is being at home with our gift. At ease. No pressure. Having nothing to prove. At home.

Next to the gift of salvation and the sure knowledge that we will go to Heaven when we die, the anointing is our most precious possession.

The anointing, then, is the Holy Spirit. It is really just another word for the Holy Spirit. It is one of John's special words for the Spirit. 'You have an anointing from the Holy One ... The anointing you received from him remains in you, and you do not need anyone to teach you' (1 John 2:20,27). Because the Holy Spirit is our teacher, he 'will teach you all things' (John 14:26) and 'will guide you into all truth' (John 16:13).

I would rather have more of this than anything. I want more of the Holy Spirit than I want anything in the world. In Proverbs the anointing is called wisdom, understanding. 'Wisdom is supreme; therefore get wisdom. Though it cost all you have, get understanding' (Prov. 4:7). James uses this word 'wisdom'. 'If any of you lacks wisdom, he should ask God, who gives generously to all without finding fault, and it will be given to him' (Jas. 1:5).

In a former generation the word was sometimes 'unction', probably because the Authorised Version uses that word in 1 John 2:20. It was often referred to regarding preaching – whether a minister preached with 'unction'. I have often said I wanted unction on my preaching, that I would push a peanut with my nose across London if that would bring it.

I said something like that one evening when I was being interviewed at Spring Harvest. Then after ten to fifteen minutes someone raised his hand and asked, 'Whatever is unction?' My first reaction was surprise, that the person might be putting me on. But I have come to see that some of us have frequently used terms that many people sincerely did not understand. I therefore want to take adequate time to explain the term in this chapter. The word 'unction' appears in the great hymn or psalm 'The King of Love my Shepherd is' which was sung at the funeral of Diana, Princess of Wales.

> Thou spread'st a table in my sight;
> Thy unction grace bestoweth:
> And O what transport of delight
> From Thy pure chalice floweth.
> *Henry W. Baker*

Jesus stood up to read in the synagogue. The scroll of the prophet Isaiah was handed to him. Unrolling it, he found the place (Isa. 61:1–2) where it is written: 'The Spirit of the Lord is on me, because he has anointed me to preach good news to the poor. He has sent me to proclaim freedom for the prisoners and recovery of sight for the blind, to release the oppressed, to proclaim the year of the Lord's favour' (Luke 4:18–19).

The word 'anointing', or 'unction', is translated from the Greek *chrisma*. I shall stick to the term 'anointing'. The dictionary definition refers merely to the application of ointment or oil. The anointing of oil, sometimes called Extreme Unction, is one of the seven sacraments of the Roman Catholic Church, generally used when a person is dying.[1] It is based on James 5:14: 'Is any one of you sick? He should call the elders of the church to pray over him and anoint him with oil in the name of the Lord.' But there is no indication this should be done only when someone is dying. In my church we have administered the anointing of oil for years and have had a number of people testify to being healed.[2]

The word comes from the root *chrio* in the Greek and is the word that underlies 'Christ', which means Messiah, or the

Anointed One. The word *chrisma* is used in 1 John 2:20,27 but is *not* the same word as 'charisma' (that usually refers to someone's electrifying personality) or even 'charismata' (which mainly refers to gifts of the Holy Spirit). And yet, as we shall see, the latter words, 'charisma' and 'charismata', are nonetheless the result of the anointing.

In the Old Testament the term 'anointing' is used in at least five ways. First, it refers to oil – olive oil that was mixed with spices: myrrh, cinnamon, cane and cassia. 'Make these into a sacred anointing oil, a fragrant blend, the work of a perfumer. It will be the sacred anointing oil' (Exod. 30:25). This oil was used to anoint the 'Tent of Meeting, the ark of the Testimony, the table and all its articles, the lampstand and its accessories, the altar of incense, the altar of burnt offering and all its utensils, and the basin with its stand. You shall consecrate them so they will be most holy, and whatever touches them will be holy' (Exod. 30:26–9). The anointing was said to be on holy things.

Second, the anointing referred to the consecration of priests. The same oil that anointed holy things was poured on Aaron's head and on his sons (Lev. 8:10–13). This was a very, very serious matter. Moses said to Aaron and his sons, 'Do not leave the entrance to the Tent of Meeting or you will die, because the LORD's anointing oil is on you' (Lev. 10:7; cf. Lev. 21:10–12). The priests had charge of the anointing oil (Num. 4:16).

Third, the anointing refers to the consecration of kings. The first occasion for this was when Samuel anointed Saul. 'Then Samuel took a flask of oil and poured it on Saul's head and kissed him, saying, "Has not the LORD anointed you leader over his inheritance?" ' (1 Sam. 10:1). For this reason Saul never ceased to be regarded as the Lord's 'anointed' (1 Sam. 24:6) even though God had rejected him from being king (1 Sam. 16:1).

Fourth, the anointing became closely connected to the

Holy Spirit. Soon after Saul was anointed by Samuel the Spirit of God came on him in power (1 Sam. 10:6), God changed Saul's heart (1 Sam. 10:9) and he prophesied (1 Sam. 10:10–11). The Spirit of God came on David later when Samuel secretly anointed him king. Saul still wore the crown but was rejected by God from being King (1 Sam. 16:1). Samuel anointed David, who had no crown. But the Holy Spirit came on him immediately. 'So Samuel took the horn of oil and anointed him in the presence of his brothers, and from that day on the Spirit of the LORD came upon David in power' (1 Sam. 16:13). It could be said that Saul had the crown but lost the anointing. 'Now the Spirit of the LORD had departed from Saul, and an evil spirit from the LORD tormented him' (1 Sam. 16:14). But David had the anointing – that is, the Holy Spirit in power – without the crown.

In this fourth use, then, emerges what has been implicit all along: the oil was a symbol of God's Holy Spirit. And yet the Holy Spirit himself manifested his power where this oil had been poured so that the anointing oil was also more than a symbol. This became obvious when Jesus sent out the twelve disciples and gave them authority over evil spirits. 'They drove out many demons and anointed many sick people with oil and healed them' (Mark 6:13). So the oil was more than a symbol; it seems to have been an instrument in some sense. This is something I do not claim to understand. Although the prayer offered in *faith* is what healed sick people, this was to be preceded by the anointing of oil (Jas. 5:14–15).

The fifth use of the word did not seem to require any oil at all. Prophets were said to be anointed.[3] 'Do not touch my anointed ones; do my prophets no harm' (Ps. 105:15). Abraham is called a prophet (Gen. 20:7) and Abimelech was warned not to harm him. This means that Abraham was anointed and yet there is no evidence that oil had been poured on him. The same seems to be true with the words of Isaiah: 'The Spirit of the Sovereign LORD is on me, because the LORD has anointed me to preach good news to the poor. He has sent me to bind up the broken-hearted, to proclaim freedom for the captives and release from darkness for the prisoners' (Isa. 61:1). This pointed to the anointing of God's Messiah, the Lord Jesus Christ, and yet I know of no reference to oil being literally poured on Jesus.

It should not surprise us that people in the Old Testament had this anointing. The Holy Spirit is 'eternal' (Heb. 9:14) which means he is God – from everlasting to everlasting, having no beginning. The descent of the Holy Spirit at Pentecost was not the beginning of the Holy Spirit any more than the birth of Jesus was the beginning of the Word, the *Logos*, the second person of the Trinity (John 1:1). What happened at Pentecost was the inauguration of the supreme manifestation of the Spirit now that Jesus had returned to the Father. But the Holy Spirit was present in the Old Testament from the beginning of creation (Gen. 1:2). As the Old Testament stalwarts did what they did by *faith* (Heb. 11:2), so likewise is the *anointing* on them – without the need of olive oil – the explanation of what they did.

The anointing is what enabled Elijah to challenge the prophets of Baal without fear on Mount Carmel, 'How long will you waver between two opinions? If the LORD is God, follow him; but if Baal is God, follow him' (1 Kgs. 18:21). Elijah was as much at ease in putting that question as he had been when he was led by the Spirit to challenge those false prophets in the first place. He was so much at home in this that he could openly ridicule them. They had shouted, 'O Baal, answer us!' He taunted them. At last he said, 'Come here to me,' and repaired the altar of the Lord. He simply prayed, 'O LORD, God of Abraham, Isaac and Israel, let it be known today that you are God in Israel and that I am your servant and have done all these things at your command.' Then the fire fell. When the people saw this they fell prostrate and cried, 'The Lord – he is God! The Lord – he is God!' (1 Kgs. 18:36,39)

The only explanation for Elijah's success: his anointing.

The anointing is what lay behind Stephen's face shining like the face of an angel and the reason the Jews could not 'stand up against his wisdom or the Spirit by whom he spoke' (Acts 6:10,15). It is the reason Moses' face was radiant (Exod. 34:30). It is why he could say to the people, 'Do not be afraid. Stand firm and you will see the deliverance the LORD will bring you today,' after which the Israelites went through the Red Sea on dry ground (Exod. 14:13,22.) The anointing is what enabled Peter, who had denied Christ to a servant girl seven weeks before, to preach to thousands of Jews on the day of Pentecost when three thousand were suddenly converted (Acts 2:14–41) and why he could say to a lame beggar, 'Silver or gold I do not have, but what I have I give you,' whereupon the man who had never walked was instantly healed (Acts 3:6–7).

In the fourth century an African by the name of Athanasius was in the minority when he held to the eternal deity of Jesus Christ. He stood alone, claiming that the Word which became flesh was co-eternal, co-substantial and co-existent with the Father. 'The world is against you,' his critics shouted at him. 'If the world is against Athanasius, Athanasius is against the world,' he retorted.

The anointing is the reason Martin Luther could turn the world upside down in the sixteenth century. He stood alone in his claims that we are justified (declared righteous) before God by faith *alone*. The Western world was never to be the same again.

The anointing is the explanation for John Calvin's *Institutes of the Christian Religion*. Dedicated to the king of France and published all over Europe, these four books did more to refine the theology of Protestantism than any other publication. Said Henry Emerson Fosdick, to read the history of Western civilisation apart from Calvin is to read it 'with one eye shut'.

The anointing is what gave courage to the Marian martyrs.

The Anointing

During the reign of Mary Tudor ('Bloody Mary', who reigned 1553–8) men gave their lives for their faith. As the flames came up over the bodies of Bishop Hugh Latimer and the young Bishop Nicholas Ridley, Latimer shouted back to Ridley, 'Fear not, Master Ridley, and play the man; we shall this day light such a candle in England that I trust shall never be put out.' A year later the martyr John Bradford could say to his friend as the flames were about to encircle their bodies, 'Be of good cheer, brother, we shall have a merry supper with the Lord tonight.'

The anointing is what gave John Wesley and George Whitefield so many conversions when they preached in the fields. It is what fell on Jonathan Edwards' hearers when he preached his sermon 'Sinners in the hands of an angry God' and strong men were seen holding on to tree trunks to keep from sliding into Hell. It is what came on thousands one Sunday morning at Cane Ridge, Kentucky, in 1801 when an unknown lay preacher stood on a fallen tree, taking his text 'We shall all stand before the judgment seat of Christ' (2 Cor. 5:10) and hundreds fell to the ground. It is sometimes called the Cane Ridge Revival – America's Second Great Awakening.

The best way I have been able to describe it, therefore, is that it is when our gift functions easily. It comes with ease. It seems natural. No working it up is needed. It is either there or it isn't. If one has to 'work it up' one has probably gone outside one's anointing. If one goes outside one's anointing the result is often fatigue – that is, weariness or spiritual lethargy that has been described as 'dying inside'.

2

Accepting our Anointing

Some years ago there was a bestseller called *The Peter Principle*. The idea in the book is that every person is promoted to the level of his or her incompetence. Either because of ambition or through the need for a vacancy to be filled, a person who has been functioning with complete ease until now is suddenly in a position in which he or she is struggling. The result is irritability and frustration; sometimes high blood pressure, nervous breakdowns and broken marriages. The way the Peter Principle works is this. A person who has been a first-rate typist or secretary may find themselves in management. As long as they were typing letters, taking dictation or answering the telephone they were superb. They coped with ease. But a vacancy at a higher level came along and they applied for and got the job. They now have to make hard decisions, handle people under them and find that they are under stress. They are not cut out for this after all – but they try to stick it out. They have been promoted to the level at which they are not able to function with ease. They should have stayed with their old job. But no. They are determined to make it work. Few people will admit they have been promoted to the level of their incompetence.

Sadly there is truth to the Peter Principle. Many people, in government, industry and the Church, have jobs or positions for which they are not qualified. They have been promoted (sometimes they promoted themselves) to the level of their incompetence. A lay preacher becomes a pastor, the pastor of a small church is determined to get the larger church, a musician becomes a worship leader, a person who speaks in tongues begins giving words of knowledge, a person who has a brilliant testimony suddenly wants to be a preacher. The examples are endless. The move to a more challenging position is often the way God in fact leads us on, but if it isn't God who does the promoting we are in trouble. Another way of putting it is: they have moved outside their anointing.

Everybody has an anointing. The Apostle Paul called it 'gifts' in 1 Corinthians 12:4–11. The Greek word *charismata* really means 'grace-gift'. It is God's gift, which he graciously bestows on those who don't deserve it. The difficulty is, ambition gets into the picture and some don't like it if their own anointing does not result in a high profile. Paul compared these grace-gifts, which I am calling anointings, to the parts of the human body.

> Now the body is not made up of one part but of many. If the foot should say, 'Because I am not a hand, I do not belong to the body,' it would not for that reason cease to be part of the body. And if the ear should say, 'Because I am not an eye, I do not belong to the body,' it would not for that reason cease to be part of the body. (1 Cor. 12:14–16)

Some anointings, then, have a high profile – like the eye or the head. Some anointings have a lower profile – like the hand or the feet. 'The eye cannot say to the hand, "I don't need you!" And the head cannot say to the feet, "I don't need you!" On the contrary, those parts of the body that seem to be weaker are indispensable' (1 Cor. 12:21–2). Some people have an anointing with no apparent profile at all – like the kidneys or intestines which are indispensable (1 Cor. 12:23ff.). God's design is that there should be 'no division in the body, but that its parts should have equal concern for each other' (1 Cor. 12:25). Paul draws a conclusion: 'Now you are the body of Christ, and each one of you is a part of it' (1 Cor. 12:27). There are those with the high profile, as apostles, prophets and teachers; some have an anointing (not listed in 1 Corinthians 12:8–10) which the Authorised Version merely calls 'helps' – 'those able to help others' (1 Cor. 12:28).

The question is, will we accept our own anointing? Or will we let ambition and personal drive for recognition get in the way? Martin Luther said that God uses sex to drive a person to marriage, ambition to drive a person to service, and fear to drive a person to faith. But if the *eros* love that may have a lot to do with making a couple want to get married is not paralleled by *agape* love (selfless concern), that marriage will eventually be on the rocks. Likewise if ambition is not paralleled by a love for the honour of God, we will make the grievous mistake of moving outside our own anointing. This is partly why Jesus asked the question: 'How can you believe if you accept praise from one another, yet make no effort to obtain the praise that comes from the only God?' (John 5:44).

We all have an anointing. We even had an anointing before we became Christians. God had his hand on each of us even before we were converted. He sent angels to us even before we ever thought about inheriting salvation. 'Are not all angels ministering spirits sent to serve those who *will* inherit salvation?' (Heb. 1:14). And yet it does not follow that only those who will become Christians have a natural gift, or anointing.

There is a very real and definite sense in which the non-Christian has an anointing. It comes from creation, combined with the influences upon him or her. It is partly hereditary, partly environmental. One gets certain gifts or abilities from parents; these are refined by education, culture and the effect people have on us. It is sometimes called 'common grace' – God's goodness to all men and women. John Calvin called it a 'special grace within nature'. Jesus said, God causes his 'sun to rise on the evil and the good, and sends rain on the righteous and the unrighteous' (Matt. 5:45). James said, 'Every good and perfect gift is from above, coming down from the Father of the heavenly lights, who does not change like shifting shadows' (Jas. 1:17).

This is why a person may be a genius even though he or she is not a Christian. God gave Albert Einstein his IQ of 212 (100 is regarded as being average, 130 or more being a genius). God enabled Edvard Greig to compose his glorious Concerto in A Minor. God gave Yehudi Menuhin his talent to play the violin. It is what enables a person to invent software in computer technology and that which gives the ability to be a programmer. It is what lies behind a brilliant surgeon who can operate on the brain, perform a liver transplant or diagnose a disease. It extends to sports, finances, architecture, literature. The explanation: God's common grace. It is distinct from saving grace. All who are saved have common grace, of course, but not all who have common grace are saved.

Two years after Louise and I married, I sold vacuum cleaners to make a living. I had been prepared for this from boyhood days. My first job at the age of ten was selling *Grit*, a weekly newspaper, door to door. Years later, selling vacuum cleaners from door to door, humbling though it was, paid the bills. I can say I had an anointing to sell vacuum cleaners as Paul had an anointing in making tents (Acts 18:3). Perhaps Paul never knew when he might have to fall back on this talent. Hardly a week goes by, to this day, that I do not wake up having dreamed that I am back in Fort Lauderdale and Miami having to sell vacuum cleaners. Sometimes God gives an anointing that is not as admirable or refined as playing a violin. But we should see that the anointing is a word that can be used a number of ways, not the least of which is that it is an enabling at the level of common grace. That was what was functioning in my vacuum cleaner days.

For this reason, every person has an anointing. It does not in itself prove one's spirituality since even the non-Christian has his own gift. It is natural. It may not stem from being born again. The genius who becomes a Christian may be of great benefit to the Church and the world, as when God saves an Athanasius or Augustine, but that genius was already there before he or she became a Christian. It is common grace.

Every saved person should come to terms with their own anointing. One should recognise to what extent that anointing is natural – that is, already there before conversion – and supernatural – that is, what God has been pleased to bestow after conversion. For example, a person with a natural public speaking ability may be called to preach soon after conversion. The person who loves to write poetry before conversion may write Christian hymns or songs after being saved. Sometimes a person who is good at languages may find him or herself very attracted to and gifted with speaking in tongues, although many who speak in tongues are ungifted in foreign languages. But the Holy Spirit often incorporates our natural abilities and superimposes great grace upon them so that they appear supernatural to others but seem natural to those who have them. This not only helps us to understand ourselves a little better, it will help us to see that a talent may have nothing to do with a fresh anointing of the Spirit that comes from walking in the light after we have been saved (1 John 1:7). It should also help us to apply it to our lives so that we do not fancy ourselves more gifted – or more spiritual – than we really are. This understanding should help us to see our usefulness, in our jobs and our understanding of ourselves as well as our usefulness in the Church.

Why is accepting our anointing so important? Because we should see that our anointing is a thing most precious. It is the way the Holy Spirit sovereignly works most freely in us. All Christians have the Holy Spirit (Rom. 8:9; 1 Cor. 12:13) but not all Christians have the same measure of faith. 'For by the grace given me I say to every one of you: Do not think of yourself more highly than you ought, but rather think of yourself with sober judgment, in accordance with the measure of faith God has given you' (Rom. 12:3). The measure, or limit, of our faith is our anointing. What may be my anointing may not be yours; what may be yours may not be mine. The question is, will you and I accept – with cheerfulness – the anointing God has given us?

Each of us must therefore come to terms with his or her particular anointing. After all, it is the Lord who sovereignly determines the anointing. I may well *wish* I had another person's anointing. Will I come to terms with the way God has chosen to work in me? Will I admit that God has given me a certain gift? Will I affirm his sovereign dealings with me? Or will I be jealous of another's gift, position or responsibility?

It is sometimes hard to admit one *does* have an anointing. We are sometimes afraid to appear immodest or vain. But God cannot use us to the full as long as we doubt what he has taken pains to give us. It is also hard, sometimes harder, to admit our limitations: that we are not as gifted or brilliant as another. I have had to admit that I am no Jonathan Edwards or Martyn Lloyd-Jones. That is painful, especially when some people feel I should be more high-powered than I am. What can we do? The only thing we can do is to get our approval from God who made us as we are and put us where we are, unworthy though we are.

Paul said, 'We, however, will not boast beyond proper limits, but will confine our boasting to the field God has assigned to us' (2 Cor. 10:13). By 'limits' he means 'measure', the same word as in Romans 12:3. By 'proper' limits he means limits God has set. He therefore acknowledges the sovereignty of God in this limitation. God made Paul as he is and determined *where* he should be. Here is a man at peace with himself; he has accepted his anointing. He is not going to go beyond

God's sovereign limit. He is not going to go beyond God's sovereign strategy. By 'boasting', Paul simply means affirming himself as God would have him do. He admits he has certain gifts.

There is great peace to the person who accepts his or her anointing, and great frustration – sometimes sorrow – to the one who does not. Some of us have ambition that is greater than our intelligence, ability or gifting. Some of us have ambition beyond what we are really good at. Some die a thousand deaths having to admit they are not cut out for this or that position. They even fall into the folly of the Peter Principle.

You have an anointing sovereignly given to you by God. You can discern exactly what it is – if you will be true to yourself. 'To thine own self be true,' said Shakespeare. This way you will not be governed by selfish ambition or governed by what you *wish* were true. In a word: the anointing is what comes easily. Your actual anointing is in easy operation when you function without fatigue. Your sphere of anointing is when you work without having to break a door down in order to walk through it. You let it open without your raising a little finger.

My favourite story in the Bible is that of Joseph (Gen. 37–50). Joseph was his father's favourite son and was given a coat of 'many colours' (AV), the NIV says a 'richly ornamented robe'. This understandably made his brothers jealous. Joseph had another gift – this one from God – which had to do with dreams. He was given prophetic dreams. 'He said to them, "Listen to this dream I had: We were binding sheaves of corn out in the field when suddenly my sheaf rose and stood upright, while your sheaves gathered round mine and bowed down to it" ' (Gen. 37:6–7). This made his brothers hate him even more. But that didn't stop the arrogant seventeen-year-old from flaunting his gift further. 'I had another dream, and this time the sun and moon and eleven stars were bowing down to me' (Gen. 37:9). It didn't take a Sigmund Freud to interpret that dream, either!

There was nothing wrong with Joseph's gift, but there was a lot wrong with Joseph. Joseph wasn't ready to use that gift; he abused the grace that accompanied it by deliberately exalting himself over his brothers. It would be a long time before Joseph could be trusted with that gift. In the meantime God, who earmarked Joseph for greatness one day, also earmarked him for a long, hard era of preparation. The Bible calls this 'chastening' (AV), or being 'disciplined' (Heb. 12:6). This word comes from a Greek word that means '*enforced learning*'. God has a way of teaching us a lesson. Joseph needed to be humbled.

Joseph's anointing, or grace-gift, needed to be refined. He needed an equal amount of grace on his gift. It was one thing to be gifted with a prophetic dream (that turned out to be absolutely accurate, see Genesis 45), but another to have grace to keep quiet about it. There was no need to tell it. Had Joseph been graced with the fruits of the Spirit, as love, joy, peace and patience (Gal. 5:22), he would not have played into the volatile feelings of his brothers. He showed no love, not a bit. But his gift still functioned.

The gifts of the Spirit are one thing, the fruits another. Sadly most of us want the gifts. One minister gave an appeal after preaching on both the gifts and the fruits of the Spirit and invited those who wanted to be prayed for to receive the gifts to come down the left aisle; those who wanted to be prayed for to receive the fruits of the Spirit were to come down the right aisle. Several dozen flocked down the left aisle, only three people came down the right aisle.

But many of us are like that. Joseph was like that. I am like that. God has had to discipline me most severely to get my attention, that I might want more of the fruits of the Spirit. He literally brought me to a place where I had no choice! And that happened to Joseph. After Joseph's brothers got rid of him by selling him to some Ishmaelites, Joseph was found working for Potiphar, an Egyptian commander. Joseph had hardly worked a day in his life but now he was a slave. He as a man was being tested to the full.

That is not all; Potiphar's wife flirted with Joseph and tried to get him to go to bed with her. After he refused again and again, she lied about him, claiming that he had tried to rape her. He was slammed into prison, and never had the future looked so bleak. He felt nothing while the angels rejoiced. It was one of his finest hours. Billy Graham said that it seems that the devil gets 75 per cent of God's best men through sexual temptation. Joseph had the chance of a 'perfect affair' – Potiphar's wife wouldn't tell, Joseph wouldn't tell and the only ones he cared about anyway, his family in Canaan, would never know. But he refused to sin against God (Gen. 39:9). He as a man passed the test. It didn't improve Joseph's gift but it refined Joseph as a man, giving him a greater measure of the fruits of the Spirit.

While in prison Joseph was being tested again. He could not have known that his two visitors in prison would do two things for him: (1) show that his gift still functioned and (2) see what measure of the fruits of the Spirit he had. On the first he passed with flying colours. The two visitors – Pharaoh's cupbearer and baker – each had dreams and Joseph interpreted them perfectly. But he failed the second test. When he prophesied that the cupbearer would get his job back in three days Joseph said, 'Remember me . . . mention me to Pharaoh . . . I have done nothing to deserve being put in a dungeon' (Gen. 40:13–15). I think Joseph's Heavenly Father looked down from Heaven and said, 'Oh Joseph, I wish you hadn't said that, you will need a couple more years in prison.' In those two years Joseph learned truly to love and to forgive.

Joseph's gift of interpreting dreams needed to be matched by an equal measure of infused grace – the fruits of the Spirit – so that his anointing could function to edify everyone, not just himself. This would be done not only by totally forgiving his brothers but by seeing how God could elevate him without Joseph having anything to do with it! It happened when Pharaoh had a dream which no one could interpret – and the cupbearer remembered Joseph. God has a way of finding us in the most unlikely places. He wants to set us free from our dungeons without our pulling strings.

A few years ago I remember watching the scene of Jim Bakker being handcuffed and put in prison. Jim had become a household name in America. His rise to fame came after we moved to England, but I had heard of his TV ministry. He was accused of misusing funds that were sent to him as a result of his appeals for people to give. When I saw him after he had been sentenced I assumed that he was getting what he deserved.

While he was in prison Jim Bakker wrote me a letter. He thanked me for my book *God Meant it for Good*.[1] This gave me pause. I had no great admiration for him but, learning that he had read my book and been helped by it, I felt ashamed I had not been more compassionate. It taught me a lesson – that I should never underestimate how God will use us, neither should we be surprised who might be touched by our ministry. It turns out that Jim Bakker was indeed changed through reading my book, and after he was out of prison, he asked to meet me should I be in America some time.

Having spent five years in prison, he came to see me in Key Largo, Florida, where we were on a fishing holiday. He told me how he hung on to a statement he read in *God Meant it for Good*: 'God's time has come when someone pleads your case (and knows all the facts) without your opening your mouth.' He had no earthly idea how that could happen to him. But without his knowing it a professor of law at an American university came to the private conclusion Bakker had not received a fair trial. This man wrote to Bakker and got permission to read the entire transcript of the trial. After considerable research this law professor became the instrument that eventually led to Bakker's early release from prison. It all happened when God sovereignly led a man Bakker had never met but who felt a compulsion to take on his case.

The anointing God gives will always be a legitimate anointing – what is just or fair; what is right. Whatever God does is just, even though we don't deserve it. Examine your own anointing. Is it not fair? He has not asked you to do what you cannot do. Your anointing will be an anointing you can use without fatigue. It comes easily. Because you can do it and you know you can do it.

For example, God will never appoint me to be a professor of mathematics in a university. Or even an algebra teacher in a high school. Many years ago, when I was looking for a way to earn a living during my long era of ecclesiastical wilderness, I was asked if I'd take a one-day job as a substitute teacher at a high school in Wurtland, Kentucky. The job would pay me $14.00 so I agreed. One of the classes I had to teach was algebra. I had never excelled in maths and I failed algebra. No problem. I just explained to the class that their teacher would return from illness tomorrow and they were to do the next two or three pages in their textbooks. This went down well – until one student after another brought me a problem asking, 'Teacher, how do you do this?' Stunned and scared I replied, 'Look here, I have my way of doing this. Your teacher no doubt has another way, and it would complicate things if I told you my way [which was no way at all] of coping with this particular algebraic formula.' That worked for a while but it turned out the next day the regular teacher was still ill and they called me back! Even more stunned and scared I repeated the above line. I think the students twigged that I didn't have a clue! I was never invited to teach there again.

But God's anointing and promotion will be legitimate – it will mean that all you have been given by creation and refined by education and culture will cohere so that you will not be stunned and scared by where he puts you. The job will be right. Your ability to function will flow. It will be because you have come to terms with your anointing. It is legitimate because God set the standard. You can achieve your goal because the standard God set is never beyond the level of your competence. There is also a legitimate basis for feeling good about yourself because you are doing what he has equipped you to do. When, therefore, you come to terms with your own anointing you can stop looking over your shoulder at another's anointing. You find a gratification in the works of your own hands – which God made possible. 'A man can do nothing better than to eat and drink and find satisfaction in his work. This too, I see, is from the hand of God, for without him, who can eat or find enjoyment?' (Eccles. 2:24–5).

> There is some place for you to fill,
> Some work for you to do,
> That no one can or ever will
> Do quite as well as you;
>
> It may lie close along your way,
> Some homely little duty
> That only needs your touch, your sway,
> To blossom into beauty.
>
> *Anonymous*

3

The Limits of our Anointing

Every anointing has its limit. Nobody can do everything. There may even be geographical limitations. We are confined to the 'field' God has assigned to us, said Paul (2 Cor. 10:13). God sets the limit on *where* we can function and also a limit to *how many gifts* we have. We must therefore learn to accept ourselves and, simply, be ourselves.

Sometimes the hardest thing in the world is to accept yourself. I have struggled immeasurably at this point. To be myself has been about the hardest thing I've sought to do in Westminster Chapel. My consolation is this: God will use me only to the extent to which I am true to what I know. This means I must not pretend to understand a verse in the Bible which remains hidden at the moment. Someone recently asked me, 'What is your eschatological position on the millennium? Are you pre-millennial (Christ comes before the millennium), post-millennial (Christ comes after the millennium) or a-millennial (no millennium at all)?' I replied that I've been right once, but I don't know when that was! At one time or other I have believed every known view on that subject. I therefore have not preached much on eschatology (the doctrine of last things). John Calvin wrote commentaries on nearly every book in the Bible but the book of Revelation; he didn't understand it.

I did not come to England to become the minister of Westminster Chapel. I was offered a place at Regent's Park College at Oxford in 1973 for the purpose of doing theological research on the Puritan John Owen, a man I had come to admire. Three years later I was invited to preach at Westminster Chapel. To my surprise I was asked to stay. But in those early years I began to take myself a bit seriously, especially if I had preached a good sermon. While compliments can be encouraging, they almost ruined me in some ways because I tried to come up to a standard that some said I met. It wasn't my standard but theirs.

It hadn't been that way at first. We had only agreed to stay for six months and therefore I didn't try to impress anybody. I was merely myself. Later on they issued the official call to be the minister. I agreed to stay. But my preaching began to change. Some said I had been shouting too loudly when I first preached, so could I please stop it. Others wanted me to sound like Dr Lloyd-Jones, who always started a sermon slowly and softly. Still others said, 'Don't tell anecdotes or refer to yourself when you preach.' When I managed to remember these things I would get praise from certain people who hinted that, just maybe, I might eventually become a worthy successor to Dr Lloyd-Jones. I came up to their standard!

But I was miserable. I already felt grossly unworthy to be there. I am not only an American but a hill-billy from Kentucky. In the days when there were only forty-eight states we had a saying, 'Thank God for Arkansas'. Kentucky was forty-seventh in educational standards, but Arkansas was below us! Now I found myself in this revered pulpit of G Campbell Morgan and Dr Martyn Lloyd-Jones. I felt I should try to be as good as they. That was when I began to take myself too seriously. I was a nervous wreck. I was now afraid to be myself – and show why some people look down on a Kentuckian.

Before I knew it I was bordering on moving outside my

anointing. If I was truly myself I was afraid people would think 'Yuk'. But if I was not myself, God would think it! I eventually came to terms with my limits – probably the hardest thing I've ever done. It became a matter of sheer obedience to God. I had to affirm him for making me as I am and affirm myself, even if people didn't like it. After all, I began to see with ever-increasing conviction, what matters is what God thinks and the way I will be regarded on the Final Day.

Have you ever wondered what it will be like at the Judgment Seat of Christ? I don't know where it will be – whether at a place on earth, in the sky or in a newly created part of God's universe. But you and I will be there. It is hard to imagine having confidence, or boldness, on that day even though John said that this is possible if 'love is made complete among us' (1 John 4:17). It seems to me that our hearts will be pounding out of our chests. Surely it will be the most sobering, terrifying moment we have ever experienced.

You and I will be judged at the Judgment Seat of Christ in part by whether or not we (1) accepted our anointing, and (2) lived within the limitations of that anointing. The reason is this. We will not be rewarded because of a gift God gave us. Joseph will not be rewarded in Heaven because he received prophetic dreams or knew how to interpret dreams. The Apostle Paul will not be rewarded in Heaven because of his high IQ. It is *obedience* that will bring a reward. 'For we must all appear before the judgment seat of Christ, that each one may receive what is due to him for the things done while in the body, whether good or bad' (2 Cor. 5:10). Whether or not we receive a reward will be determined by our *accepting* our anointing (which requires obedience) and *living within its limitations* (which means not disobeying), whatever the profile that follows.

We will also be blessed here below on the basis of how we lived within the grace given to us. We may or may not be pleased with the profile that comes with that anointing. But the greatest thing that can happen to you or me at the Judgment Seat of Christ is to hear Jesus say, 'Well done.' And to the degree we accept and live within that anointing *now* we can feel God say, 'Well done.' It is a wonderful feeling that comes from knowing you please God. Not man. God. And it is within the grasp of every single one of us.

God never promotes us to the level of our incompetence. What he truly calls us to do, we can do. As St Augustine prayed, 'Command what Thou wilt; give what Thou commandest.' God *always* provides grace for what he has called us to do. 'Your strength will equal your days' (Deut. 33:25). If you or I are operating at a level that brings fatigue and leads to what some now call 'burn-out', something has gone wrong; we moved outside our anointing at some stage. It should never happen.

This is not to deny that God may hide his face from us. It is not uncommon to experience the 'dark night of the soul'. But this is not necessarily the same thing as burn-out. God may leave us to test us, as he did Hezekiah, 'to know everything that was in his heart' (2 Chron. 32:31). But burn-out is what we bring on ourselves by taking on what God did not command.

The Apostle Paul came to terms with his limitations and strengths. He demonstrated this when his enemies scoffed, 'His letters are weighty and forceful, but in person he is unimpressive and his speaking amounts to nothing' (2 Cor. 10:10). That stung. It hurt. He implicitly acknowledged nonetheless that his public speaking probably did not flow with the eloquence of a trained orator. 'I may not be a trained speaker, but I do have knowledge' (2 Cor. 11:6). Paul thus spoke with disarming frankness, and yet he was obviously no Uriah Heep – 'I do have knowledge.'

Paul's opponents, at least some of them, were apparently professionally trained in oratory. To the sophisticated Greek at the time, skill in rhetoric provided a commendation that was thought superior to all others. The Greeks loved the orator, the man who could carry people with eloquence and words. That to the Greek was a big plus, and the one who had this gift had a head start over everybody else. Paul conceded that he had not been trained in the refinements of rhetoric; as P E Hughes puts it, the 'alluring tricks of oratory were not his stock in trade'. Not that Paul was not an able preacher – he was, and had many converts. But he was no Cicero.

'But I do have knowledge,' he could say. He may not have been a trained speaker but he knew what he was talking about. He *was* trained – in the Law; he sat at the feet of Gamaliel, the greatest tutor of his generation (Acts 22:3). And as it happened his expertise touched on the *very issue* that had become the focus at the time: the place of the Law in the Christian life. So his anointing came through where it counted. It turned out he *had* the training that mattered. To Paul's opponents the issue was *how* you said it; to Paul the issue was *what* you said. In a word: Paul's anointing of knowledge more than compensated for his deficiency in public speaking. Paul did not feel deprived, nor was he threatened. Truth was more important than style, the message was more important than the method; doctrine was more important than one's delivery. The issue to him was the content of the Gospel.

There are some lessons here for you and me. First, as I said already, nobody has everything. That is enough to keep all of us humble. But there is another lesson: for every limit there is a compensation. You may not have the gift you envy in another, but God has given you an anointing that person probably does not have. Rachel was loved by Jacob, but Leah produced the children (Gen. 29:17, 31ff.). God has a way of compensating all of us when we feel so deprived. He gives anointings to each of us in the Body of Christ 'just as he wanted them to be' (1 Cor. 12:18). 'God has combined the members of the body and has given greater honour to the parts that lacked it, so that there should be no division in the body, but that its parts should have equal concern for each other' (1 Cor. 12:24–5).

God has decided what our own particular anointing should be. Although not all of us have Jeremiah's anointing, as surely as we have been put into the body of his Son we have this in common: 'Before I formed you in the womb I knew you, before you were born I set you apart' (Jer. 1:5).

It does not follow that each of us will automatically accept the limits of that anointing and remain obedient. As we will see later, King Saul was given a special anointing but abused it – and became yesterday's man overnight. In other words, Saul became irrelevant. A has-been. Until that happened he was today's man – the man of the hour. He had a lively anointing that indicated God's approval. But by taking himself too seriously and letting his success and stature go to his head he moved *outside the limit* of his anointing, and God didn't like it one bit. Saul became yesterday's man. Overnight.

What happened to Saul could happen to you or me. It was even the Apostle Paul's greatest fear. 'Therefore I do not run like a man running aimlessly; I do not fight like a man beating the air. No, I beat my body and make it my slave so that after I have preached to others, I myself will not be disqualified for the prize' (1 Cor. 9:26–7). Paul feared being yesterday's man.

So it does not follow that we will not abuse this trust. Many have abused it indeed, brought disgrace on the name of Christ and left many sincere Christians bewildered. God is jealous for his own glory and jealous with regard to our anointing. As long as we affirm what he has given and live within it – never moving beyond it – he will continue to bless us and ensure we do not become yesterday's man or woman. But he does not show favouritism and will not bend the rules for any of us. For all I know King Saul may have believed in the 'divine right of kings' before it became an assumption over four hundred years ago. The idea was that a monarch has a divine and indefeasible right to his or her kingship and authority; for a subject to rebel against the sovereign was the worst of political crimes. But the monarch was also above the law of the land, it was believed, and King Saul seems to have thought this when he *moved outside his anointing* and assumed the prerogatives of a priest (1 Sam. 13:9–14).

Saul promoted himself to an anointing that was not his anointing at all. It was Samuel's. Samuel was called to offer a sacrifice to God. Not Saul. Not the king, however important he was. Samuel had put Saul in the kingship but Saul began believing he, as king, could do *anything* he chose to do. Wrong. He was still to remember there were things *others* were called to do without him. Some of us want to do everything. Some of us think we can do anything. Saul became impatient because Samuel didn't turn up on schedule, so he went ahead and did Samuel's job. 'He waited for seven days, the time set by Samuel; but Samuel did not come to Gilgal, and Saul's men began to scatter. So he said, "Bring me the burnt offering and the fellowship offerings." And Saul offered up the burnt offering' (1 Sam. 13:8–9). When Samuel did finally arrive he was horrified that Saul had moved outside his own anointing.

> 'You acted foolishly,' Samuel said. 'You have not kept the command the LORD your God gave you; if you had, he would have established your kingdom over Israel for all time. But now your kingdom will not endure; the LORD has sought out a man after his own heart and appointed him leader of his people, because you have not kept the LORD's command.' (1 Sam. 13:13–14)

Saul learned immediately that God did not give him indemnity because of his position; he would be judged and evaluated as any other human being. God can bring down a monarch, a TV evangelist, a minister – whether he be minister of a mega-church or vicar in a local parish.

This is scary. I could become yesterday's man overnight. It

is my worst nightmare. When I see what has happened to men and women abler than I, and then I know all too well what I am, I ask: am I next?

Is there a way you and I can ensure our present anointing will not become yesterday's anointing? I believe there is and that is partly why I wrote this book. Please believe me when I say in utter candour that I spoke to myself in every line I wrote. I don't want what has happened to others to happen to me. I therefore wrote with all earnestness that you and I may enjoy a daily *fresh* anointing that will preserve us from the folly of becoming yesterday's servant!

When Paul said we should not think of ourselves more highly than we ought to think he explained how we can do this: by accepting the 'measure', that is, limit, of our faith. Some have more faith than others. It can be painful to have to admit how limited our faith is.

I once asked Brother Andrew, famed for smuggling Bibles into Communist countries, 'How many Bibles should I take into Russia?' He replied, 'As many as your faith lets you.' He went on to say, 'Some can take two hundred, some only a hundred.' I had been invited by two American professors to join them in a trip to the Soviet Union in 1974. I had been told that the agents at the border would not search my body but only our suitcases, so I took two Bibles in my jacket. That was the extent of my faith.

We must accept the limits of our anointing in the same way. We may have an unrealistic expectation of what we ought to be able to do. The problem is, some of us have a higher expectation of ourselves than God has of us. He knows our frame, 'remembers that we are dust' (Ps. 103:14). But if we have had a high dose of ambition spoon-fed to us from childhood (sometimes from demanding parents), we may feel frustrated that we accept such low limits for ourselves. But there is great peace, I say, when we come to terms with our limitations.

I went to Oxford in 1973 with the express purpose of writing a thesis on the Puritan John Owen's view of the priestly work of Christ, a subject suggested to me by Dr J I Packer. My supervisor at Oxford, Dr Barrie White, was quite happy for me to do this. His early assignments had me reading Owen's pre-history, getting to know the main Puritans who preceded him, that I might be able to understand who shaped Owen's theology. At the end of my first year Dr White and Dr Packer called me in for a conference. They looked sober. They looked at each other and asked, 'Shall you tell him, or shall I?' By that time I was getting worried. Dr Packer began to speak. As tactfully as he could he said I should 'minimise my liabilities' and concentrate on what my first year at Oxford suggested I was good at. The bottom line: I should forget about doing a thesis on John Owen. I rushed home to our house in Headington, Oxford, and went to bed with a severe migraine. I never felt so humiliated and embarrassed in my life. 'What will my friends think? What will they think back in America when they hear I came to Oxford to do a thesis on John Owen but had to pick a different subject?'

It was the best thing that could have happened to me while at Oxford. It took a few weeks before I fully accepted my limitations. But I began to see the wisdom of Jim Packer and Barrie White, and concentrated on what I was good at. What I ended up doing changed my life!

When we live within the limitations of our anointing there is freedom. Where the Spirit of the Lord is, there is liberty (2 Cor. 3:17). As my friend Pete Cantrell says, 'The greatest liberty is having nothing to prove.' I have discerned by trial and error that the more conscious I am of God's presence the more I feel like being myself. The less conscious I am of his presence the more I feel the need to prove myself. But the more I am myself the greater my liberty. This is because I am affirming God, who made me as I am. When I move outside my anointing I am trespassing. When I try to mimic somebody else I am stealing another's anointing and it always backfires on me.

The funny thing is, when I try to imitate someone else I never capture their real genius but their eccentricity. It is a fact that what is most easily copied in any man or woman is their odd manner or even their weakness.

A well-known Texas preacher of a previous generation had an eccentric habit of cupping his left hand over his ear when he began to soar in his preaching. Nobody knew why he did it. Young ministers all over Texas and Oklahoma would do the same thing; when they thought they were ringing the bell the left hand would come up over the ear. They thought they had the anointing! As it happened they made that same man professors of preaching at Southwestern Baptist Theological Seminary in Fort Worth, Texas. You could always tell one of his students!

Now I told the above story *at* Southwestern Baptist Theological Seminary a few years ago. I did it to see if I could find out why the old preacher did that. It worked. One of the older professors came up to me afterwards. 'I know exactly who you are talking about,' he said.

'But why on earth did he do that with his left hand over his ear?' I asked.

'Because he was hard of hearing,' came the answer. 'He could hear his own voice better.'

Hardly the anointing. But when anybody begins to imitate another who happens to have a great anointing, that person will not get the true anointing but will ape his eccentricity. Dr Lloyd-Jones told me of a man in Wales years ago who had the habit of shaking his head back to keep hair from falling over his eyes. Sure enough, said Dr Lloyd-Jones, there were young men all over Wales who would shake their heads as they preached – one was even bald-headed!

God made each of us as we are. He chose our parents before we were born, chose our environment, our childhood peers, shaped our interests – not to mention determining our IQ! When we come to terms with our limitations we gain not only peace but productivity in the end. We will do a thousand times more by accepting our limitations than we will by being governed by unrealistic expectations on un-warranted ambitions, and trying to prove how clever we are. 'It is he who made us, and we are his' (Ps. 100:3). 'But now, this is what the LORD says – he who created you, O Jacob, he who formed you, O Israel: "Fear not, for I have redeemed you; I have summoned you by name; you are mine" ' (Isa. 43:1).

A while ago I heard Professor Thomas F Torrance of Edinburgh give a lecture. It ranged from contemporary theology to nuclear physics. He took questions from the audience that included professors of various backgrounds. There was not a single question Dr Torrance could not answer. I could see why Karl Barth called him the most learned man in Europe. I don't think I was ever so impressed at one man's learning and intellect.

I wanted to be like Torrance. I aspired to read philosophy and master Einstein's theory of relativity. I wanted to know every theologian of the twentieth century backwards and forwards. I wanted to be able to answer those professors in nuclear physics, as Torrance did. Then I remembered I had failed algebra and couldn't answer simple questions from those high school students in Wurtland, Kentucky. I knew I was no T F Torrance and never would be.

Accepting our limitations is essential to accepting our anointing. Perhaps God will not use us as long as we have unrealistic aspirations for ourselves. This unrealistic expectation has its origin in our pride. 'And I saw that all labour and all achievement spring from man's envy of his neighbour. This too is meaningless, a chasing after the wind' (Eccles. 4:4). I was not being true to myself or the way God made me by entertaining such lofty notions. I was only wanting to make my peers envious by my accomplishments.

At the Judgment Seat of Christ the truth about all of us will come out. There will be no pretence then. It is best to accept our limitations now and stop pretending now. And God will begin to use us. There will be productivity in the end and peace all along. That peace compensates immeasurably for the folly of pretence we had to give up.

YESTERDAY'S
ANOINTING

4

Yesterday's Anointing

I was brought up in the Church of the Nazarene, a denomination that was born in revival. There was an unusual anointing of convicting power on that church in its early days. They had what its founder, Phineas Bressee, called 'the glory'. What was that? It was the anointing that transcended their lack of education, money, refinement and prestige; the presence of God was at times so powerful that it seemed almost impossible for lost people to enter their services without getting converted. People who came to laugh and scoff ended up smitten and on their knees in tears before God. The services were frequently characterised by shouts of joy and people waving their handkerchiefs with inexpressible happiness. In my home town of Ashland, Kentucky, we were called 'Noisyrenes'. It was a stigma I felt in school when classmates knew where I went to church. But it was my church's genius. In his last days old Dr Bressee would preach from church to church one message: 'Keep the glory down'. Why? He knew that if they ever lost it they were finished. They had nothing else going for them at the time – money, schooling, prestige. But they had the 'glory' – the anointing.

This shows yet another aspect of the anointing. It is when the Holy Spirit himself comes down *on* a people. It is when the Spirit himself is allowed to take over. He bypasses education, culture and prestige. It is when one's refinement virtually counts for nothing. The Spirit, in a word, is himself. The result is that people do things and feel things they had not expected. It is what Dr Bressee meant by the 'glory'. It convicts sinners who had not wanted to be convicted. Or converted. It may bring great joy – when people laugh, shout or fall to the floor having lost strength. Jonathan Edwards called it 'swooning'. It happened at Cane Ridge. It happened with the early Nazarenes.

Sometimes we sing the hymn in our church: 'Have Thine own Way, Lord, have Thine own Way'. I wonder if God looks down on us incredulously and says, 'Really?' If he had his way indeed, what would happen? I don't know. I know how he has worked in the past. The trouble is, our education, culture and refinement *stand in the way* of the Spirit having his own way. Old Dr Bressee feared that Nazarenes might one day become like this and lose the 'glory'.

But there is a problem with this. Should the anointing lift and the glory fade away, there are always those who sadly won't admit to this withdrawal of the Spirit. And they 'work it up' – creating the shouting and manifestations that become pale imitations. Once this happens the glory becomes yesterday's anointing – in two ways. First, God may not necessarily want his glory to be manifested in precisely the same way as it had been unveiled in a previous era. Yesterday's anointing was real enough, but it was for yesterday. Second, those who 'work it up' are trying to keep yesterday's anointing alive and the flesh becomes all too obvious. They are trying to re-live what God was doing yesterday but may not have chosen to do today.

I was converted on Easter morning in 1942, aged six and a half, at my parents' bedside. At the age of nineteen I felt the call to preach and became pastor of a small country church in the mountains of east Tennessee. What I described above came a year later – 31 October 1955 – when I was also a student at Trevecca Nazarene College. I was driving in my car from

Palmer to Nashville, when the glory of the Lord filled the car. I felt that surge of the Spirit go into my chest like liquid fire.

What happened was this. I had turned off my car radio and decided to pray for the rest of the journey. I had an extreme heaviness in my chest and stomach but had no idea at the time that God was at work. I felt the opposite. God seemed a thousand miles away. Two scriptures, however came to me at once: 'My yoke is easy and my burden is light' (Matt. 11:30), which was the opposite to the way I felt, and 'Casting all your care upon him, for he careth for you' (1 Pet. 5:7 AV), which I pleaded to be able to do. All of a sudden, I saw the Lord Jesus interceding for me at God's right hand. It was powerful, almost overwhelming. The next thing I remember was hearing the voices of the Son and the Father which issued in the sweetest peace and rest of soul. It was incredible. It was even physical – that is, I felt the *warmth* of the Spirit in my chest.

The Lord Jesus was more real to me than anything or anyone else. An anointing came on me that opened the scriptures in a powerful but lucid manner. My theology changed. I had a series of visions. I saw that I would one day have an international ministry. The peace and joy and sense of God in those days was extraordinary. I have no doubt that it, together with things I had seen in my old church, prepared me to be open to the Spirit at the present time.

What I have described above are two examples of yesterday's anointing: what my old denomination and other revival eras were like and what once happened to me. The anointing on my former denomination was very real and powerful. But the possibility remains that it is but a memory. There is no guarantee that it will continue. What happened to me on 31 October 1955 was very real and powerful but a year later it was largely a memory. I could never forget what happened to me and the memory of it can be very edifying. In fact I can almost re-live the experience when I ponder it. However, the truth is that bitterness came in within a year and the peace and joy were no longer real and powerful.

It is not always easy to know why the Spirit subsides after a while. One cannot blame Dr Bressee for wanting to 'keep the glory down'. For when it lifts things are not the same. I only know that the manifestation of God's glory in this life will tend to be temporary. Revivals end. Why? I go back to the two aforementioned reasons. First, me. Us. We grieve the Spirit. The chief way we grieve the Spirit seems to be bitterness. Because right after Paul said, 'And do not grieve the Holy Spirit of God, with whom you were sealed for the day of redemption' (Eph. 4:30), he added, 'Get rid of all bitterness, rage and anger, brawling and slander, along with every form of malice. Be kind and compassionate to one another, forgiving each other, just as in Christ God forgave you' (Eph. 4:31–2). I do know that in my own case bitterness and an unforgiving spirit crept in and the powerful sense of God's presence subsided.

But the second reason is the sovereignty of the Spirit. He chooses to stay for a while, but not indefinitely in the sense he had been manifesting himself. Why? You tell me. I only know that the Holy Spirit is sovereign and, whether he is grieved or if it belongs to his inscrutability, he doesn't stay around indefinitely. Sometimes it is for years and sometimes it is for days. One hopes the immediate sense of his power will last, but eventually the Holy Spirit seems to withdraw the feeling of awe.

My point is this. We need to come to terms with what may suddenly become yesterday's anointing. It will do us no good to pretend that what happened yesterday is happening today if it isn't.

Dr Lloyd-Jones told me this story. In his former church in Wales a man stood up to read the scriptures in a Monday evening prayer meeting. The Spirit came on him in an extraordinary manner. It seemed as if the meeting would go on and on into the night, it was so wonderful. But Dr Lloyd-

Jones eventually closed the meeting (he told me he worried for years that he shouldn't have). The following Monday night the same man tried it again. Dr Lloyd-Jones said, 'I knew he'd try to do it again and I knew what would happen.' It didn't happen. You cannot make yesterday's anointing today's anointing if the Spirit isn't willing.

I have had to come to terms with yesterday's anointing at more than one level. Church history, speaking generally, is like a graph on a chart going up and down! There are high-water marks and times when the situation was bleak. One of the more important lessons for us is to see that God does not always repeat himself when manifesting his glory. God was powerfully at work in men like Luther and Calvin in the sixteenth century. He was powerfully at work in men like Wesley and Whitefield in the eighteenth century. But the manifestations of his glory were quite different, when you compare the two eras.

To over-simplify, what God did in the sixteenth century was largely cerebral: that is, glorious doctrines were rediscovered – justification by faith alone, assurance of salvation by looking to Christ alone. Not that people didn't experience these truths – they did, and the world was turned upside down. But the preaching of Wesley and Whitefield was largely experiential. The immediate witness of the Spirit accompanied conversions. Some manifestations included falling to the ground. 'Swooning' or 'losing one's strength' was Jonathan Edwards's way of putting it.

The Welsh Revival (1904–5) was quite different. There was a lot of singing, many people giving testimonies and great joy. Not a lot of preaching, however. But the power present was undeniable. Dr Lloyd-Jones also told me this story. A coal miner came home from work only to find that his wife had gone to church without cooking his meal. He was angry. He said to himself, 'I will go to that church and break up that meeting.' When he arrived he couldn't get in because the place was packed and people were crowded at the door. He was sufficiently livid not to be put off. He managed to push through the crowded doorway and get inside. The next thing he remembered was finding himself on his knees in front of the pulpit with his hands in the air, crying to God for mercy! The people who witnessed the scene said that once he got inside he walked on the tops of each pew making his way to the front where he was gloriously converted.

I call that power. Anointing. What memories came out of the Welsh Revival! But when it was over, it was over. It became yesterday's anointing. Sadly, some people can only conceive of revival in terms of the anointing that was in Wales in those days. One London pastor wrote me a firm letter rebuking me for my openness to a particular man's ministry. He said, 'When revival comes to London, *I'll* know it.' Really?

We must recognise that yesterday's anointing was momentous. When God turned Saul into another man it was momentous and when Saul prophesied it was momentous. They said, 'Is Saul also among the prophets?' (1 Sam. 10:9–11). It was a wonderful moment in Israel and a pivotal moment for Saul.

But often what is momentous doesn't last. While reminding one of the glory of yesterday, it can become but a bare resemblance of yesterday. In the case of King Saul he could still prophesy after the Spirit of God departed from him. He was coasting along on the momentum of yesterday's anointing. Certain manifestations of an authentic work of God can repeat themselves somehow after the anointing has in fact diminished.

Because the gifts and calling of God are 'irrevocable' (Rom. 11:29) a person who had a tremendous anointing yesterday can continue to see the momentum of that anointing continuing to manifest itself. He or she may hastily conclude that 'the anointing is still with us' when it is but the momentum of yesterday's anointing.

This is sobering. I could be a hypocrite in my personal life and yet my gift could continue to function. I could even deceive myself by telling myself, 'I must be right with God or I couldn't preach.' The truth is, God's calling and gifts are irrevocable. That means that God will not withdraw my preaching gift simply because I have not been a loyal, obedient son. He gave me certain abilities when he made me and called me into the ministry. By study and hard work I can improve upon those gifts – *without* a fresh anointing that comes *only* from continued intimacy with God. And when people say, 'That was a good word,' or 'God spoke to me through you today,' I could assume that God is very pleased with me indeed. One of the worst things we can do is to take compliments too seriously.

It is possible that there are those who sincerely *don't* know better. They are well equipped, high-powered, eloquent and charismatic; people are blessed by their ministries. These people who are thus used of God may sincerely believe they are pleasing God because their anointing is functioning so well. 'I am under God's anointing,' they may well say. True. But it could be yesterday's anointing. There may be nothing fresh about it.

This explains how a TV evangelist can preach against sin (and the people stand in awe and give their contributions) and be living in sin himself the whole time. Until the minister is found out his anointing blesses people. It is a genuine anointing, mind you. It is real and powerful. But it is yesterday's anointing.

What is wrong with that? A lot. God knows what is going on, and after a while he may decide to blow the whistle on us. Not that he isn't interested in our ministries or in our being a blessing to people. He is. But he is also jealous of that anointing, and if it is not replenished by a *fresh* anointing that only comes from a life of intimacy with him, total obedience, walking in all the light and seeking his face daily, he is unhappy.

After a while he may decide, 'enough is enough', and put us in the category of yesterday's man or woman.

That is what happened to King Saul. He became yesterday's man but continued to wear the crown. He was yesterday's man – a has-been – but continued to prophesy. He was yesterday's man but still had influence and power. He was coasting on yesterday's anointing. But he forfeited the fresh anointing that comes from unfeigned obedience.

It is sad to see those in places of power who are almost certainly living on the prestige of yesterday's anointing. It can happen to a pastor, a bishop, a preacher or any church leader. One may have the ear of thousands but not the ear of God. One may have a great mailing list and exert influence but not be the mouthpiece of the Holy Spirit.

The fresh anointing is the essential thing. It is what replenishes the irrevocable. If our irrevocable anointing (Rom. 11:29) is not replenished by a fresh touch of God, we are depending on yesterday's anointing.

A poll was taken not long ago that revealed how much time the average clergyman or church leader actually spent alone with God in prayer and private devotions every day. The average: four minutes a day. We may wonder why the Church is powerless, generally speaking, but this is part of the reason for the spirit of death on the Church. Listen to these words that come from Martin Luther's journal: 'I have a very busy day today. Must spend not two, but three, hours in prayer.' John Wesley prayed no less than two hours every day. But there aren't many John Wesleys out there, are there? Or Martin Luthers.

This analogy fits every church member as well as every church leader. You may be in business, the media or law; you may be high-powered in what you do. You may be making money and living comfortably. You notice how God supplies your needs and how he guides your life and blesses you. Don't be deceived. You too can do all this on yesterday's anointing –

feeling very good about yourself but cold inside. You may say, 'I can't be all bad, look how God is with me.' True. But yesterday's anointing can do all that. You need intimacy with God as much as any church leader, whether you are a nurse, a housewife, a lorry driver, taxi driver or dentist. God is no respecter of persons. He won't bend the rules for any of us. He wants obedience, intimacy, a daily seeking of his face, a building up of a deposit account. 'Do not store up for yourselves treasures on earth, where moth and rust destroy, and where thieves break in and steal. But store up for yourselves treasures in heaven, where moth and rust do not destroy, and where thieves do not break in and steal. For where your treasure is, there your heart will be also' (Matt. 6:19–21).

A deposit account in heaven, however, does not merely include how much we give in terms of money to the Kingdom. It also includes our forgiving one another. The greater the offence we have to forgive, the greater the *credit* to our account! In fact Jesus uses that word three times in Luke 6:32–6:

> If you love those who love you, what credit is that to you? Even 'sinners' love those who love them. And if you do good to those who are good to you, what credit is that to you? Even 'sinners' do that. And if you lend to those from whom you expect repayment, what credit is that to you? Even 'sinners' lend to 'sinners', expecting to be repaid in full. But love your enemies, do good to them, and lend to them without expecting to get anything back. Then your reward will be great, and you will be sons of the Most High, because he is kind to the ungrateful and wicked. Be merciful, just as your Father is merciful.

The 'credit' is given to us here below as well – by a fresh anointing.

Our reward in heaven will not be determined by yesterday's

anointing but by today's *fresh* anointing. 'For we must all appear before the judgment seat of Christ, that each one may receive what is due to him for the things done while in the body, whether good or bad' (2 Cor. 5:10). I will not receive a reward for how well I preached, how many thousands I reached or blessed, or even how many people were converted under my ministry. God does this by virtue of the grace he endued me with by creation, environment, experience and the gifts he gave me when he called me to preach. To be rewarded for my *gifts* is nonsense! 'For who makes you different from anyone else? What do you have that you did not receive? And if you did receive it, why do you boast as though you did not?' (1 Cor. 4:7). God is not going to reward me for the ability he alone gave me. My reward in Heaven (may God grant that there is such) will come *entirely* by whether I practised what I preach: walking in the light, dignifying the trial, totally forgiving others and placing utmost priority on my intimacy with him.

And yet my *continued* effectiveness here below is also determined by my hearing God's voice today. If my anointing given me yesterday is replenished by a fresh anointing that comes by the way I live personally and privately, I will continue to hear God speak and will know his will daily. I will not miss what he wants of me or what he wants me to see around me. I will not miss what God is in – what he is doing, where he is moving and the way he sovereignly chooses to manifest his glory. I can think of nothing worse than missing out on what God is doing. And yet my knowledge of the Bible will not in and of itself guarantee that I will recognise what he is up to today.

We must all learn to distinguish the difference between what is important and what is essential – and always do the latter. Whether with our use of time, money, our diaries and social relationships, the issue is what is essential and being sure we do what is *essential*. Yesterday's anointing is important;

today's *fresh* anointing is essential. If I do not experience a fresh anointing every day it is only a matter of time before I will become yesterday's man.

Dr Paul Cain uses an expression, 'No camping allowed'. By this he means to warn people not to stop and 'camp' at the phenomenon of manifestations. For example, he reckons that Pentecostal churches and many charismatic churches focused on speaking in tongues and never really wanted to move beyond this. He fears equally that those who were touched by the Toronto Blessing of laughing and falling on the floor are quite happy to live in this kind of atmosphere indefinitely. It is a danger every movement faces. They get stuck into a particular manifestation of God's glory and want to perpetuate that manifestation rather than be open to the many ways God may yet manifest his glory. A particular manifestation can become yesterday's anointing very quickly, but there will be those who want to 'camp' at one kind of phenomenon.

Dr Cain goes even further. He says while some see an emergence of a new denomination as what began in revival, the truth is that the new denomination being formed is more likely the end of the revival. Once people try to organise themselves around a new movement of the Spirit they unwittingly render that movement yesterday's anointing.

An example of this is the aftermath of the Cane Ridge Revival of the early nineteenth century in Kentucky. Witnesses at the time, when the move of the Spirit first broke out, marvelled at the way in which heated debates over theological and denominational differences meant almost nothing. Baptists, Presbyterians and Methodists, for example, did not feel the need to argue with one another over the differences that had previously divided them. They just rejoiced in God and his Son. What mattered, all felt, was that they were *Christians* – nothing more. But, lo and behold, a leader in the Cane Ridge Revival came up with the idea of starting a 'Christian' church! And what do you suppose happened? A new denomination began – they called it the Christian Church! The revival was virtually over. It became yesterday's anointing overnight.

One of the hardest lessons for us to learn is that we cannot monopolise the Holy Spirit. We cannot get a corner on the 'Holy Spirit market'. He is not for sale and will not allow himself to be franchised like a fast food chain. We must therefore reverence him, honour him, let him be himself; we must flow with him and not try to coerce him to flow with us. Otherwise he will back off – very quietly and imperceptibly – while we carry on our way, like Joseph and Mary on their way back to Galilee, assuming the Lord was with them (Luke 2:46–8). He wasn't. They had to go back and look for him until they found him. That is what we have to do.

5

Yesterday's Man or Woman

The LORD said to Samuel, 'How long will you mourn for Saul, since I have rejected him as king over Israel? Fill your horn with oil and be on your way; I am sending you to Jesse of Bethlehem. I have chosen one of his sons to be king.' (1 Sam. 16:1)

I was not prepared for my normal Bible reading when I turned to 1 Samuel 16 on 24 August. I follow a Bible reading plan devised by the Scottish preacher Robert Murray M'Cheyne which was first introduced to me by Dr Martyn Lloyd-Jones. I had read that passage dozens of times. I had preached through 1 Samuel three times since becoming a preacher of the Gospel. But when I read 1 Samuel 16:1 that day it was as though a laser beam flashing from three different directions illuminated that verse with a clarity that shook me rigid. In one verse I saw three types of ministry: yesterday's man or woman – King Saul; today's man or woman – Samuel, to whom God was speaking; tomorrow's man or woman – David, whom Samuel was led to anoint.

King Saul, yesterday's man, lost God's approval but still wore the crown. Tomorrow's man, David, got the anointing but without the crown. Today's man had to break with yesterday's man and cast his lot with tomorrow's man. It was a hard and painful word which Samuel was having to receive. It shows the sobering responsibility on the shoulders of the one who is truly today's man or woman.

In recent years I have found myself using the expression 'yesterday's man'. I'm not sure where I heard it first. I have understood it to mean a person who ceases to be relevant. He or she may continue to minister and say things. But such a person has somehow 'lost' it – they are out of touch. They are saying the same old thing they have uttered in years gone by when it probably had some impact if not power. But it has ceased to carry weight today. Such a person often struggles to prove him or herself, trying to show their relevance. But the power has gone. In a word: such is a has-been although they are still around.

With King Saul, it was a case of losing God's approval. 'I have rejected him as king over Israel,' God said to Samuel. And yet Saul's kingship went on for *twenty more years*. The *anointing* was given to David who had to *wait for the crown* for twenty more years. But he had the anointing that mattered. Saul would continue to be regarded as the Lord's 'anointed' by David because Samuel had anointed Saul as king. As long as Saul was king, David called him the Lord's 'anointed' (1 Sam. 24:6; 26:9). But David had the anointing that mattered for he had God's own approval. 'From that day on the Spirit of the LORD came on David in power' (1 Sam. 16:13).

Saul kept an anointing nonetheless, in two ways. First, he still maintained the kingship publicly. Secretly God had rejected him and yet Saul still had the platform and influence. Second, he still retained certain gifts with which he was endowed when he had been turned into another person. God had changed his heart some time before (1 Sam. 10:9) and he was equipped with an extraordinary gift of prophecy. The Spirit of God came on him with power and he prophesied. Those who witnessed it asked each other, 'Is Saul also among the prophets?' (1 Sam. 10:11). Long *after* God had rejected Saul *he still had the same gift* and people were still saying, 'Is

Saul also among the prophets?' (1 Sam. 19:24). This helps to explain why Paul the Apostle could say, 'For God's gifts and his call are irrevocable' (Rom. 11:29). In spite of Saul's high-handed disobedience, God did not take back the gifts that were bestowed upon him.

Saul's example shows how a person in a place of influence and power can still wield tremendous respect publicly but secretly be rejected by God. David's example shows how a person can have no platform but have God's approval.

I knew a man years ago who possibly had the greatest anointing of oratory and eloquence I ever heard. He was a pastor, pulpiteer *par excellence* and Bible scholar. But something happened to him spiritually that indicated he wasn't right with God. Ambition took over. He wanted to be a denominational man rather than a man of God. Climbing the ecclesiastical ladder became more important to him than revival – once his greatest passion. And yet this was not generally known of him; the public perception of him was that he was a godly, anointed man. Being one of his greatest supporters (I would call him an equivalent of Saul), I warned him that he was losing something very precious.

Previously three other men had begun to pray spontaneously with an intense burden for this oratorical pastor-scholar. The next day these men began to prophesy publicly. One cried out, 'Ichabod has been written over this church.' As he spoke a haze filled the place, then left. A feeling of awe swept over the people, although they did not have a clue what it meant. Afterwards the men prophesied privately to this church leader. He rejected their word, almost mocking them. They departed with heavy hearts.

This event I have just described made a profound impression on me. It was pivotal for my future. I was one of the few who had access to this occasion. The pastor who rejected the words of the brothers was deeply admired by me. He had tremendous influence on me as a young minister. I knew, however, that this revered man of God had lost something precious – a fresh anointing – but hardly anyone noticed it at the time.

It was a good number of years before it became obvious that God had departed from him and that church. He maintained his pastorate, kept his platform and influence, preached with skill and got the respectability and promotion he apparently so desperately wanted. But he lost the anointing that mattered. That church lost its glory in its quest for respectability. Today it bears no resemblance to its former glory.

And yet it took years before this loss of glory was widely recognised. Immediately after the men prophesied to the pastor nothing happened; that is, he continued to preach, the church continued to thrive – with 'Ichabod' written over it. Like a fallen tree whose leaves stay green for a while, so the absence of the fresh anointing was not evident for years.

But in God's sight this eloquent preacher was yesterday's man before the people generally would know it.

Saul's example explains how some continue in ministry and dazzle thousands, but only by an 'irrevocable' anointing which God graciously does not take back. Such a person may function with considerable brilliance but does so because the public has not discerned what God knows. Only Samuel knew the truth. Saul was yesterday's man but functioned on and on by virtue of his prestige and position plus the irrevocable gifts with which his calling had been endowed.

When I was a boy growing up, I became enamoured with the powerful preachers who came to my church, which was regarded as rather strategic in my denomination and tended to attract the most gifted evangelists. Imagine my dismay when I found out how some of them lived private lives of sexual immorality while ministering at the same time. Dozens and dozens of people were converted by their ministries and yet they lived secret lives of sheer hypocrisy. God's gifts are irrevocable.

I knew yet another man (he too was a hero to me) who could preach with such power that people trembled as he spoke. He could describe sin and its perils with such graphic language that its effect on me was to get as far from sin as possible. When he would give the appeal after his sermon people ran to the front with great conviction. He could depict Hell with such descriptive language that one could almost smell the brimstone. It turned out that a woman (not his wife) who followed him from town to town, booking into the same hotels, was his lover. It seemed not to affect his preaching at all.

King Saul had a good beginning. Samuel had devoted himself to finding Israel's king. Saul was Samuel's discovery. Not only had God given Saul a new heart and other gifts, he took the reins in early days which showed an authority that electrified the people. When the people were on the brink of being demoralised Saul took charge.

> The Spirit of God came upon him in power, and he burned with anger. He took a pair of oxen, cut them into pieces, and sent the pieces by messengers throughout Israel, proclaiming, 'This is what will be done to the oxen of anyone who does not follow Saul and Samuel.' Then the terror of the LORD fell on the people, and they turned out as one man. When Saul mustered them at Bezek, the men of Israel numbered three hundred thousand and the men of Judah thirty thousand. (1 Sam. 11:6–8)

Who would have thought that in a short time God would have to say to Samuel, 'How long will you mourn for Saul, since I have rejected him as king over Israel?' (1 Sam. 16:1)? *At the age of forty Saul was yesterday's man.*

What went wrong? Saul began to take himself too seriously. He did not wait for Samuel to offer the burnt offering and fellowship offerings (1 Sam. 13:8–9). He went outside his anointing – he decided to offer those sacrifices. This was Samuel's prerogative alone. But Saul assumed that he as king could do whatever he pleased, so he did. He offered up the burnt offering. At that moment Samuel arrived. 'What have you done?' Samuel asked (1 Sam. 13:11). Saul explained, justifying himself, 'You did not come at the set time . . . I felt compelled to offer the burnt offering' (1 Sam. 13:11–12).

'You acted foolishly,' Samuel said. 'You have not kept the command the LORD your God gave you; if you had, he would have established your kingdom over Israel for all time. But now your kingdom will not endure; the LORD has sought out a man after his own heart and appointed leader of his people, because you have not kept the LORD's command.' (1 Sam. 13:13–14)

Despite this strong word it would seem that God nonetheless gave Saul a second chance.

Samuel said to Saul, 'I am the one the LORD sent to anoint you king over his people Israel; so listen now to the message from the LORD. This is what the LORD Almighty says:"I will punish the Amalekites for what they did to Israel when they waylaid them as they came up from Egypt. Now go, attack the Amalekites and totally destroy everything that belongs to them. Do not spare them; put to death men and women, children and infants, cattle and sheep, camels and donkeys." ' (1 Sam. 15:1–3)

But Saul took himself too seriously again. He thought his own idea of sparing 'the best of the sheep and cattle' made better sense. Wrong.

But Samuel replied: 'Does the LORD delight in burnt offerings and sacrifices as much as in obeying the voice of the LORD? To obey is better than sacrifice, and to heed is better than the fat of rams. For rebellion is like the sin of divination, and arrogance like the evil of idolatry. Because you have rejected the word of the LORD, he has rejected you as king.' (1 Sam. 15:22–3)

Saul's second folly ratified his first flagrant act. It was upon the heels of this disobedience that God spoke to Samuel and told him to anoint the next king.

I can think of nothing worse than being made yesterday's man while I am still preaching and writing. We may all become yesterday's man or woman in the sense that our time to pass the truth to another generation may come. And we must die some day. But even this need not make us yesterday's man or woman. It was said of Abel, 'By faith he still speaks, even though he is dead' (Heb. 11:4). Thousands of people of previous generations still speak to the Church. But that is not what I mean by being made yesterday's man or woman.

Yesterday's man or woman is one whose loss of fresh anointing is not generally apparent. A has-been in God's sight, such a person thrives with their natural skills, grace-gifts, strong personality and influential platform, and leads many people. But God has secretly decided to pass the greater anointing to tomorrow's man or woman.

It could happen to any of us, it need not happen to any of us. One of the reasons I wrote this book is to issue a warning to those of us in leadership that we must not take our anointing for granted. God is a jealous God. 'Be careful not to forget the covenant of the LORD your God that he made with you; do not make for yourselves an idol in the form of anything the LORD your God has forbidden. For the LORD your God is a consuming fire, a jealous God' (Deut. 4:23–4).

We all at times think we are the exception to the rule. We also like to think we have a 'special' relationship with God that means we do not always have to come under his word.

This feeling stems from a self-love principle that is deceiving and deadly. It would be a long time before Saul came to terms with what Samuel knew and told him. Much later on he said, 'Surely I have acted like a fool and have erred greatly' (1 Sam. 26:21). He eventually admitted, 'God has turned away from me. He no longer answers me' (1 Sam. 28:15).

But there is another way we can become yesterday's man or woman – when we are found out. Getting caught. Exposed. When our high-handed arrogance and disregard for God's word catches up with us.

And yet, paradoxically, there is more hope for this kind of yesterday's man than when God renders us so. Getting 'caught' may mean God isn't finished with us yet! Jonah was exposed by the sailors on the ship when he was trying to run from God (Jonah 1:9ff.), but mercifully God came to him 'a second time' (Jonah 3:1). So we must *not* understand yesterday's man or woman to be in that sad state permanently. Saul was, Jonah wasn't. One can be put on the shelf and come back. But Saul didn't.

So being yesterday's man or woman may be a temporary state. It may mean a time of severe chastening, or disciplining (Heb. 12:6). God may set one on his 'back burner' until he deems us ready to be used again. Many have returned to a high profile in ministry having learned their lesson. Samson did (Judg. 16:24–30).

The obvious question is, what determines the difference? The answer, in a word: our attitude towards his rebuke. Saul was defensive and unteachable. Jonah and Samson prayed with all their hearts for another chance – and God gave it.

We may be put on the shelf, then, by our own folly. It was Paul's greatest fear at one time. 'No, I beat my body and make it my slave so that after I have preached to others, I myself will not be disqualified for the prize' (1 Cor. 9:27). There is more than one way this could happen. The man I was named after, Dr R T Williams, used to warn those whom he had just ordained to the ministry: 'Beware of two things – money and women,' he would say. 'If you are involved in a scandal with either of these, God may forgive you but the people won't.'

But people do sometimes forgive. Some think that Richard Nixon could have gone to the nation in tears and repentance and possibly would even have kept his job. One TV evangelist, instead of shedding buckets of tears publicly but defending himself to his ecclesiastical authorities privately, might have eventually won a measure of respect. But he dug in his heels, refused to take being disciplined as he should have, and will probably remain yesterday's man for the rest of his life.

David got caught for his adultery and murder after Nathan the prophet revealed the sin to him. What he did was reprehensible. But when Nathan nailed him to the wall, David took the word with both hands. Nathan said,

> This is what the LORD says: 'Out of your own household I am going to bring calamity upon you. Before your very eyes I will take your wives and give them to one who is close to you, and he will lie with your wives in broad daylight. You did it in secret, but I will do this thing in broad daylight before all Israel.' (2 Sam. 12:11–12)

This was not a very pleasant thing to hear. But David's immediate reaction was what Saul came up with too late. For David said, 'I have sinned against the LORD' (2 Sam. 12:13). David paid dearly for his sin but God wasn't finished with him. He still had a future.

A few years ago I preached on the life of David. After eighteen months in the series, when I had completed 2 Samuel 12, I lost heart. I couldn't bring myself to go on and shared my dismay with our deacons. I fasted a few days later and God unexpectedly turned up. He spoke to me clearly in almost these very words: 'So you're not going to continue preaching on the life of David?' I had decided not to do so because I didn't have the stomach to deal with the 'down' side of David's extraordinary life – when so many bad things happened and he had so little to look forward to. But God continued to speak: 'Don't you know that that is where most of your people are?' I wasn't prepared for this. I wanted to assume most of our people were godly and blameless and would find 2 Samuel 13 to 24 quite irrelevant to them. I still don't know (and am not sure I want to know) what God knew about my church, but I continued preaching on the 'down' side of David. I can tell you, it was the best part of the series! I think I had more anointing, more insight and greater liberty than ever!

David became yesterday's man only for a while. But King Saul remained yesterday's man. David was docile and tender; Saul was arrogant and hard.

The way we can become yesterday's man or woman is by losing touch with God. This was Saul's error. He lost touch with God by putting himself above the word. God did not bend the rules for the first king of Israel. He wouldn't bend the rules for certain TV evangelists. He won't bend the rules for you or me. His name and reputation don't ultimately ride on my success or failure. He can raise someone else overnight to replace any of us.

One evidence that we may have lost touch with God is by imagining that we are still on the cutting edge of what God is doing today merely because we defend what God was doing yesterday. Some may think they are in the battle because they are 'sound' theologically. Jonathan Edwards therefore taught us that the task of every generation is to discover in which direction the Sovereign Redeemer is moving, then move in that direction.

We may assume God is with us today just because he was with us yesterday. God of course promised never to leave us or forsake us. But his special presence that flows from his approval is not necessarily guaranteed. This, if I may refer to the incident again, was something Joseph and Mary learned. 'After the Feast was over, while his parents were returning home, the boy Jesus stayed behind in Jerusalem, but they were unaware of it. Thinking he was in their company, they travelled on for a day. Then they began looking for him among their friends and relatives' (Luke 2:43–4).

We may have been raised up for a particular message or mission that God was behind in a previous day, but which has served its purpose. Some ministries outlive their usefulness. Some Christian organisations outlive their usefulness. It takes an awful lot of courage and integrity to admit that a ministry may be over because it did all that it was ever going to do. John the Baptist was a sovereign vessel. But some of his followers would not accept that even he *gladly* became yesterday's man (John 3:26). John had the honesty to admit the purpose and temporary nature of his own anointing and urged his followers to embrace the One he had been raised up to prepare people for.

We may keep a platform but lose the anointing that matters – God's current approval that issues in a fresh renewal of his glory. We may enjoy a high profile, a wide following, have access to a great mailing list, exercise influence and shape opinions – all without God's current approval.

6

When Success comes too Soon

Another indication that one is yesterday's man or woman may be that success has come too soon. Everybody wants success but it can be dangerous, even leading to our becoming yesterday's man or woman – especially if it has come too soon.

You may not be conscious that you are yesterday's man or woman, especially if you are successful. It has been said, 'You can always tell a successful man, but you can't tell him much.' Such people aren't very teachable. They are not open to the notion that they are not relevant or are no threat to Satan. Some fancy they are today's men and women and live in a dream world, supposing that they are on today's cutting edge.

And yet I am not sure which is more painful – to be today's man or tomorrow's man. As we will see below, today's man often has the discomfort of breaking with yesterday's man or woman. Today's man or woman takes risks not only by cutting him or herself off from those with whom he or she was involved but also by *affirming* that which nobody knows or trusts at the time. That is what Samuel had to do.

If you are tomorrow's man or woman you must have the patience to wait for your time to come. The anointing is on you now, but you have no platform, no people, no authority or opportunity. All you can do is to wait. You have a vision that you *will* be used. But you must wait. You may have a message burning in you but your time has not come. 'Like the trampling of a mighty army,' said Victor Hugo, 'so is the force of an idea whose time has come.' That could be paraphrased: like the trampling of a mighty army so is the power of one's anointing whose time has come.

Tomorrow's man or woman has the anointing but not the platform. He or she has no basis of power in terms of recognition. They may have to await further training, further preparation and further disciplining under God's hand. Spurgeon said, 'If I knew I had twenty-five years left to live, I'd spend twenty of it in preparation.' Most people today spurn further preparation; they think they are ready now.

In early 1956 I felt that God gave me a fresh message to preach. I saw things in scripture that I had not heard preached anywhere. I saw teaching and doctrine and insight that I thought had been revealed to nobody but the Apostle Paul! I foolishly left college since I felt I had no more to learn there. I also was convinced that the Second Coming of Jesus was so near that I was wasting my time with further preparation.

In the summer of 1956 Billy Ball, a friend of mine, and I felt led to have an evangelistic meeting in a big tent. Two businessmen put up $2,000 to buy the tent. It seated a thousand. We erected a big sign near the tent on a highway in Ohio across the river from Ashland, Kentucky: TRI-STATE EVANGELISTIC CAMPAIGN. We got on the radio to advertise the mission. We purchased a thousand folding chairs. There was plenty of parking space near the tent. On the first night fifteen people arrived! We preached night after night, alternating the ministerial responsibility, the sermons lasting a good hour each time. We managed for three or four weeks. The maximum attendance on any one night was around twenty-five. More listened from their cars out of curiosity than came into the tent. It was a humiliating fiasco.

My dad was distraught that his only son, named after his favourite preacher Dr R T Williams, had come to this. A year before, my grandmother had bought a new 1955 Chevrolet and gave it to me, as I was the first Kendall in the family to be a preacher. That summer she took the car back. Dad begged for proof I was in God's will – with my strange new doctrine (to him) and the apparent lack of God's approval on my life at the time.

I assured him God was going to use me – powerfully and *internationally*! I had been given visions from the Lord that showed me clearly that I would see great revival. Dad had one question: when? I replied with absolute confidence: within one year. He asked me to write it down so he could have it to show me one year later! I wrote it down. One year later I was selling Stroll-o-chairs, a portable assortment of baby equipment that I sold to parents of newly born babies. I had no opportunities to preach. With a measure of success in making money I became interested in material things. I decided I would learn to fly. I bought a Cessna aeroplane and a new car – a 1958 Ford Edsel. I bought a new stereo and expensive clothes. I was also several thousand dollars in debt. With such a promising beginning two years before but now having to stay in secular work to pay my bills, one could say that tomorrow's man became yesterday's man in record time. It would be a long, long time before I would be in a solid preaching ministry.

So when I came to Westminster Chapel twenty years later, with university degrees under my belt, I thought, 'Now I'm ready.' I think also that my Heavenly Father looked down from Heaven and said, 'Really?' Little did I know that I was at the beginning of a ministry that would be heart-breaking year after year, preaching to three or four hundred in an auditorium that was built to seat two thousand. But at least it did my dad proud, since I occupied G Campbell Morgan's old pulpit. Now I certainly do not want to underestimate the hope that God has used me over the past twenty-one years. But if I were honest I'd have to say it has been largely preparation.

Dr Lloyd-Jones once said to me, 'The worst thing that can happen to a man is to succeed before he is ready.' He said that on one of those Thursday mornings when I was welcomed by him every week to discuss my preaching for the following weekend. I am one of the most blessed men to have had the privilege of his loving counsel. But that statement was probably the most powerful word he ever gave me. I believe it to be true and I can only conclude that I have been withheld the success I had hoped for by God's gracious will. I have sincerely prayed that God will *not* bless me with great success until he sees that I am not taking myself too seriously.

The man or woman who takes himself or herself *too seriously* is a ripe candidate for becoming yesterday's man or woman. One reason I took myself too seriously back in 1956 was that I received visions that indicated I would be used of God. I assumed these visions would be fulfilled soon. They weren't. But because I had them and believed they were truly from the Holy Spirit I assumed I was special. I became arrogant. I was not unlike Joseph, who not only strutted around in his coat of many colours but flaunted his prophetic dreams to his brothers. Those dreams *were* from God. There was nothing wrong with Joseph's gift but there was a lot wrong with Joseph. God had earmarked Joseph for a wonderful ministry down the road, but he *also* earmarked Joseph for a long era of preparation and being refined. Because Joseph was not ready. I was not ready. If you put me under a lie detector today I would have to admit I'm still not sure I'm ready for the anointing I pray for. I am still being dealt with. Like peeling the layers of an onion, so I see so much about myself that is not right.

I am so thankful God is still peeling away those layers of arrogance and presumption. I'd rather not be greatly used at all than be given a greater anointing that I would abuse. God has withheld the success I have hoped for for my own good – to keep me from being successful before I am ready. After all, what can be worse than losing God's approval and fresh anointing even though one's ministry continues as though nothing has happened? As it was put above, if the Holy Spirit were completely withdrawn from the Church today, 90 per cent of the work of the Church would go right on as though nothing had happened. It can happen to a denomination, to a local church and to an individual. That is what happened to King Saul.

A good beginning does not guarantee a good ending. King Saul had a good beginning. He did not have a good ending.

'It's not over 'till it's over,' says Yogi Bear. The cartoon character was taken from Yogi Berra, the great baseball catcher of the New York Yankees. He made famous the expression, 'It's not over 'till it's over' because many times a team could be ahead and lose at the last minute. As Rob Parsons says, 'It's the second half that counts' – not what the score is at the end of the first half. Many Wimbledon tennis championships have been lost despite a player being ahead with three championship points at forty-love. Many a promising church leader appeared to be the man of the time only to become yesterday's man overnight.

Age is not necessarily relevant in this matter. Yesterday's man may be young (Saul was forty when he lost God's approval). Moses was not ready until he was eighty. The issue is not one's age but the coalescence of two things: one's obedience and God's timing. We may be today's or tomorrow's man or woman at any age.

To chronicle Saul's life once he was rejected by God is a melancholy enterprise. 'Now the Spirit of the LORD had departed from Saul, and an evil spirit from the LORD tormented him' (1 Sam. 16:14). David's first job after his fresh anointing was to use his talent as a harpist to play for King

Saul. It gave temporary relief (1 Sam. 16:23) but only that. Little did David know that the king who held on to the crown would become his enemy and that that enemy would be the main means of his preparation for his own kingship one day.

After David's spectacular success in slaying Goliath the people came from all the towns of Israel to meet Saul and sang: 'Saul has slain his thousands, and David his tens of thousands' (1 Sam. 18:7). This may or may not have pleased David, but by their actions God was guaranteeing that David would not succeed before he was ready. 'And from that time on Saul kept a jealous eye on David' (1 Sam. 18:9).

King Saul was successful before he was ready. Many a young rock star crashed on the rock of success because they were too immature to handle the fame and the quick money. Many a young movie star became an overnight success only to lose their families and friends. Many a businessman went to the top in making money, only to lose his wife, integrity and health. I have even watched young preachers get big churches and it go to their heads and they lose the fresh anointing they once had. Success is dangerous.

Why does God allow a person to succeed before he or she is ready for it? I only know that it is a painful blessing if God withholds success from us before we can cope with it. We have all watched those movie stars, rock singers, TV personalities and even politicians who are sudden wonders overnight, only to pass behind a cloud just as soon. Or it may be that stardom and fame continue *while* the person of that renown finds he cannot handle money or resist the temptation to sex and drugs. Elvis Presley is an example of one who became successful before he was ready.

As for Saul, the idea of kingship was not God's idea. It was God's concession to a rebellious people. At the end of the day the prophet Hosea summed it up: 'So in my anger I gave you a king, and in my wrath I took him away' (Hos. 13:11). Sadly

King Saul was a part of an unspiritual people who wanted what God did not want. It was as much a judgment upon Israel as it was on Saul. And yet God gave even Saul a second chance to obey. God does not give us a word if there isn't hope.

So despite Saul's folly in not waiting for Samuel and going outside his anointing, a second chance was on offer. Notice how it was put: 'Samuel said to Saul, "I am the one the LORD sent to anoint you king over his people Israel; *so listen now* to the message from the LORD" ' (1 Sam. 15:1). Had the king truly been sorry and repentant he would have taken that word from Samuel with both hands. He should have been able to see that God was still on speaking terms with him.

If God gives us a word of rebuke we should welcome it. It may come from reading the Bible, when we least expect it. It may come through preaching. It may come from a trusted friend. 'Wounds from a friend can be trusted' (Prov. 27:6). It may come from a person with a true prophetic gift. Dr Paul Cain has given us a number of warnings. I have taken every single one of them seriously.

But what if we reject – or neglect – a word given to us and later wish we had listened? I answer: should God speak *at all* after that, take it to heart with all your being. How kind God was to come again to Saul, speaking to him with dignity. It was Saul's second opportunity after he blew it the first time. Any word from the Lord is a test. We should treat it as though we may never hear him again *just in case* we have not been fully obedient previously.

God is so gracious. Consider how angry he was years later with King Ahab. God said to Ahab, 'I am going to bring disaster on you. I will consume your descendants and cut off from Ahab every last male in Israel – slave or free. I will make your house like that of Jeroboam son of Nebat and that of Baasha son of Ahijah, because you have provoked me to anger and have caused Israel to sin' (1 Kgs. 21:21–2). Those words were apparently final and unchanging, offering Ahab no hope whatsoever. But their impact upon Ahab was profound. 'When Ahab heard these words, he tore his clothes, put on sackcloth and fasted. He lay in sackcloth and went around meekly' (1 Kgs. 21:27). That is what King Saul might have done. We might wish he had. For God is a gracious God. I doubt Elijah was prepared for what God said next about Ahab. 'Then the word of the LORD came to Elijah the Tishbite: "Have you noticed how Ahab has humbled himself before me? Because he has humbled himself, I will not bring this disaster in his day, but I will bring it on his house in the days of his son" ' (1 Kgs. 21:28–9).

The key thing is to hear God's voice. The writer of Hebrews feared that these Hebrew Christians would repeat the sin of Israel in the desert:

So, as the Holy Spirit says:
'Today, if you hear his voice,
  do not harden your hearts
as you did in the rebellion,
  during the time of testing in the desert,
where your fathers tested and tried me
  and for forty years saw what I did.
That is why I was angry with that generation,
  and I said, "Their hearts are always going astray,
  and they have not known my ways."
So I declared on oath in my anger,
  "They shall never enter my rest." '

(Heb. 3:7–11)

The writer of Hebrews warned that these Christians had become 'dull of hearing' (Heb. 5:11 AV, which is a literal translation of the Greek). In other words, they could hear but only just. He didn't want them to become stone-deaf and therefore unable to be renewed again to repentance:

> It is impossible for those who have once been enlightened, who have tasted the heavenly gift, who have shared in the Holy Spirit, who have tasted the goodness of the word of God and the powers of the coming age, if they fall away, to be brought back to repentance, because to their loss they are crucifying the Son of God all over again and subjecting him to public disgrace. (Heb. 6:4–6)

A few years ago when on holiday in Florida my wife punctured an eardrum. She was so upset that this should happen to her. We all wonder why God permits any kind of an accident. But on the first Sunday back in Westminster Chapel she happened to be sitting next to a deaf woman who had come to our church for the first time. In a few moments, as though it were a revelation, Louise felt a keen desire to learn sign language. We now have a signing ministry to the deaf in our church in which she plays a significant part. But we have learned a bit about deafness: there are degrees of deafness. Often it begins with the need of a hearing aid, then a stronger one. One wants to avoid the worst – stone-deafness, when one no longer hears at all.

This can happen spiritually. The early stage is 'dull of hearing', the worst is being spiritually stone-deaf. When one no longer hears from God it is impossible to be renewed again to repentance. Being granted repentance, what Paul calls being changed 'from glory to glory' (2 Cor. 3:18 AV), is the proof we are hearing God. He deals with us, shows us our sin, we repent and walk in the light and know sweet fellowship (1 John 1:7).

It seems to me that Saul eventually became stone deaf. God 'no longer answers me' (1 Sam. 28:15), said Saul, perhaps some of the saddest words in the Bible. When Saul said, 'no longer' he implied God used to talk to him. But not now. Saul is an example of yesterday's man who stayed in that state. It doesn't need to happen to you or me.

God sent Samuel to Saul a second time and said, 'Now go, attack the Amalekites and totally destroy everything that belongs to them. Do not spare them; put to death men and women, children and infants, cattle and sheep, camels and donkeys' (1 Sam. 15:3). This was obviously a hard word. It is one of the most difficult things in the Old Testament for many of us to take on board. And yet, though this would not be an easy thing for Saul to understand and to carry out, God coming to him a second time – giving him a second chance – should have thrilled him to his fingertips. He should have taken that word seriously and carried it out. But no. Saul thought he knew better and as a consequence of his second folly he ratified Samuel's previous word.

This convinces me that to fall into a Hebrews 6:4–6 situation one has had ample opportunity to avoid such a destiny. The way God came to Saul yet again convinces me that a person who falls – like Saul – so that he cannot be renewed again to repentance has had ample warnings and opportunities to avoid such a destiny. It is not merely being overtaken in a fault (Gal. 6:1), slipping into bad habits or company for a time, not being all that we could be for the Lord. God forgave me for my being enamoured with material things and going foolishly into debt.

Jim Bakker, the TV minister who spent five years in prison, is a forgiven man. Jim believes that it was God himself who put him in prison. But his failure was not like those described in Hebrews 6:4–6 who couldn't be renewed again to repentance. God is gracious. One doesn't trip or fall into the category described in Hebrews 6:4–6, until God's warnings have been *deliberately* and *consciously* rejected.

How may you know you are *not* stone-deaf like those in Hebrews 6:4–6? I answer: *that you hear God speak to you*. When, for example, he graciously comes to you with a word you once found too hard to take on board – but this time you accept it with both hands. God came to Jonah a second time with the same exact word that had been spurned: 'Go to the great city of Nineveh and proclaim to it the message I give you' (Jonah 3:1; cf. Jonah 1:1–2). And Jonah obeyed. As long as we hear God speak, however hard that word may seem, and we receive it gladly, we may be sure we are not yesterday's man or woman. It means God is still on speaking terms with you. Even if it is a grave warning, at least you can hear! The gravest warnings in the New Testament are in Hebrews, to those not yet stone-deaf but – at least at the time – hard of hearing. 'If any hear my voice, do not harden your heart.'

If any of us has any fear of being yesterday's man or woman, there is something we can do – now. That is to go on bended knee to a gracious God and repent of any and every known disobedience, and wait with bated breath for any second chance from him. For any subsequent word will indicate we are still on speaking terms with him, that there is still hope and that we are not stone-deaf.

There are other signs of being yesterday's man or woman. The first is when we are obsessed with one person, with jealous feelings. This was an ominous sign that Saul was losing all presence of mind. He could not cope with the people's admiration of David. The people exclaimed, 'Saul has slain his thousands, and David his tens of thousands' (1 Sam. 18:7).

Saul could not cope with a possible rival. 'Saul was very angry; this refrain galled him. "They have credited David with tens of thousands," he thought, "but me with only thousands. What more can he get but the kingdom?"' (1 Sam. 18:8–9).

If I find myself jealous of another person, either because of their success or at the possibility of their becoming a rival, or if I'm envious of their gifting, I am in a precarious state. Jealousy – the sin nobody talks about – is the downfall of many a gifted person. It blinds. It eats on one's spirit. It consumes our thoughts. It seems right at the time. It ruined Saul.

Second, a sign of being yesterday's man or woman is that I

begin trying to destroy another's credibility. Saul's one aim was to destroy David (1 Sam. 18:10–11; 19:11–23; 23:7–29). He worried more about David at times than he did Israel's enemy the Philistines. He would rather eliminate a rival than uphold the safety of God's people! Once a person begins to attack another – whether in person or in print – they fit the blueprint for being yesterday's man then and there. They may not feel a thing in their heart. When we grieve the Spirit it is usually painless. We tell ourselves we are doing God's will! But God silently and secretly withdraws the fresh anointing that could have been ours once we are obsessed with reducing another's credibility by damaging their reputation.

Third, we fear another's anointing. 'Saul was afraid of David, because the LORD was with David but had left Saul' (1 Sam. 18:12). Perfect love casts out fear; when we are afraid we are not made perfect in love (1 John 4:18). Why would anybody be afraid of another's anointing? It is God who gave it. We should affirm the anointing in another. If we are afraid of it, it suggests a rival spirit has crept in. Or we are afraid people will be influenced and think more of them than of us. We *may* be afraid that God will use that person to bring revival! We say we want revival – until, that is, it appears it won't come through us, via our party line or through those who agree with us.

The fear of another's anointing is a dead give-away that we are not right in ourselves. It characterised Saul who was already yesterday's man by that time. May God give us such objectivity about ourselves that we truly and unfeignedly confess our sin. I say again, I can think of nothing worse than for God to be in something or someone and for me not to see it. Fear keeps us from seeing the obvious.

Fourth, we could be yesterday's man or woman if we set a trap for the one who threatens us. The way Saul did it was to challenge David to fight the Philistines. 'Saul replied, "Say to David, 'The king wants no other price for the bride than a

hundred Philistine foreskins, to take revenge on his enemies." '
Saul's plan was to have David fall by the hands of the
Philistines' (1 Sam. 18:25). If I set a trap for one who is a
threat to me, I am taking vengeance into my own hands. I
render myself yesterday's man once I stoop to this. Saul's doing
this was a dead give-away that the fresh anointing was no
longer on him.

I have watched those who were threatened by another's
anointing (not that they would ever admit it was the anointing
that actually threatened them) and how they were so sure that
person would slip and be his own undoing. 'Give him enough
rope and he'll hang himself,' they would say, hoping this man
or woman would get found out – as Saul was so sure David
would never return alive from fighting the Philistines. The
truth is, David killed two hundred Philistines! When you are
hoping your enemy will trip and fall (as opposed to praying
for him or her – Matthew 5:44), you may well be on the
brink of becoming yesterday's man or woman while your
enemy is in fact God's anointed.

Fifth, when we cannot keep our word, not to mention a
vow, it shows we have lost integrity. Keeping one's word –
honesty – should surely be taken for granted. It should go
without saying that we do not tell lies, that we are honest, that
we keep our word.

Jonathan pleaded with his father Saul to spare David's life.
Then 'Saul listened to Jonathan and took this oath: "As surely
as the LORD lives, David will not be put to death" ' (1 Sam.
19:6). In ancient times the oath was the ultimate and absolute
evidence of trustworthiness. If you doubted someone's word
you could always believe them if they swore an oath! Saul did
that to Jonathan. And yet in no time, 'an evil spirit from the
LORD came upon Saul as he was sitting in his house with his
spear in his hand. While David was playing the harp,
Saul tried to pin him to the wall with his spear, but David
eluded him as Saul drove the spear into the wall. That

night David made good his escape' (1 Sam. 19:9–10).

That is how low Saul sank. He had no integrity whatsoever. The person who becomes yesterday's man or woman and stone-deaf to the Spirit almost always loses clear thinking. In the end such a person will believe a lie (2 Thess. 2:11), even as Saul sought out the witch of Endor (1 Sam. 28:7ff.).

All of us must come to terms with an unchanging fact: none of us is above God's word. We all like to think we are God's favourites. Even David, a man after God's own heart, was not exempt from God's awesome jealousy for the truth.

I do not want to become yesterday's man. I do not want to be on the shelf either. God has been so patient with me – I am so very indebted to him for his patience.

If we have had a measure of success and did not handle it well, and tripped, God may give us a second chance as well. He came to Jonah a second time with the same word as before (Jonah 3:1; cf. Jonah 1:1–2). It was the happiest word Jonah ever heard. As long as we can *hear* God's voice there is hope that we have not had success too soon and that there is more to come.

TODAY'S
ANOINTING

7

The Stigma of the Anointing

Most of us do not want the feeling of being irrelevant. We want to feel we are in touch with what is going on. We want to feel that what we have to say relates to the present scene, that we are equipped for what is needed today. The most horrible feeling in the world must be that one is yesterday's man or woman, once used but not relevant now.

The task of every generation is to discover in which direction the Sovereign Redeemer is moving, then to move in that direction. I therefore can think of nothing worse than for God to be at work and for me not to see it, for his anointing to be on someone's ministry and for me not to recognise it. The trouble is we all have an inclination to believe 'the old [wine] is better' (Luke 5:39). For example, we like what is familiar, the old hymns or songs we became accustomed to, the old style of preaching we grew up with. In a word: where there is no stigma (offence).

The word 'stigma' is a pure Greek word, *stigma*, found in Galatians 6:17: 'I bear in my body the *marks* of Jesus.' It comes from *stizo*, which means 'to prick', 'tattoo' or 'mark' as with a sharp instrument. In the ancient Hellenistic world, it was often a brand burned on the body with a hot iron which became a distinguishing mark. A man who bore the *stigma* was everywhere regarded as dishonest. It was usually marked on slaves, for running away, stealing or for some other transgression. But Paul was not ashamed of the stigma; to him it showed he was a slave of Jesus. It may have referred to his wounds or scars (cf. 2 Cor. 11:23–5). It is also somewhat synonymous with the Greek word *skandalon* – 'offence': 'We preach Christ crucified: a *stumbling-block* to Jews' (1 Cor. 1:23). 'If I am still preaching circumcision, why am I still being persecuted? In that case the *offence* of the cross has been abolished' (Gal. 5:11).

The first church of which I was pastor was in Palmer, Tennessee. I was nineteen, still a student at Trevecca. Although I came from the hills of Kentucky, where the preaching style was often loud and emotional, I did not develop a preaching style that was popular then. I have often wondered why, since most of my peers at the time preached in a way that pleased the older people: noisy, shouting as if you were losing your breath. It didn't matter whether there was any content in your sermon, a certain style largely determined whether you were acceptable. They called it the 'holy tone', maybe just a bit like what the Welsh would call the *hwyl*. When I took the pastorate of my church in Palmer, that is the style the people were used to – and wanted. When I later heard the man who founded the church literally yelling his lungs out and audibly gasping for breath after every single sentence, I wondered why they ever called me. They honestly equated the style with the anointing. I repeat, it didn't matter what you said as long as that rough, spontaneous (the less preparation, the better) style was there. It would never go down in Britain today but it was the 'old wine' to which they were accustomed. For all I knew, perhaps in a previous era, truly anointed men developed that manner of preaching. But by the time I was around it was only a form of godliness with no power. And no stigma.

The kind of preaching many like to this day, whether they are from Kentucky or an English public school, is often cultural in taste – nothing more, nothing less – a particular style with which people are familiar and which alone will be accepted. It is a certain *form* that is wanted, whatever plays into our nostalgic world. It has nothing to do with spirituality, godliness or anointing. Like people who come to church because they like the sound of an organ. Or guitar. Or architectural style. Or liturgy. As long as there is no stigma.

I am a very nostalgic person. I love walking down memory lane. A few years ago I was being driven to the airport at Cincinnati, Ohio. On the way I caught a glimpse of the old railway station in Cincinnati. When I was a boy we always had to change trains there when travelling from Ashland to my grandparents in Illinois. I spent many hours in that station when I was young. I asked the driver, 'Would you mind if we drove over to the old Union Station?' as we called it, once known as the busiest and most beautiful station in America. He was happy to do so. I got out, walked inside. It is no longer a railway station but a shopping centre! Nevertheless it was the same old building. I began to walk around, stared at the ceiling, the walls and the place where we used to eat. My heart began to pound, I found myself breathing more heavily and caught myself audibly moaning, 'Ummm . . . ummm . . . ummm.' It was almost like a spiritual experience. I could hardly tear myself away from that place. I all but wept! 'This is silly of me,' I said to myself, and I returned to the car.

Now I wouldn't have missed doing that for anything in the world. It did me a power of good. And yet it was sheer nostalgia – there was nothing spiritual about it at all. It was a precious memory being relived. Like eating 'shuck beans' and corn bread as we used to have in Kentucky. I'd walk miles to eat those again!

But it taught me a lesson. Not only can we not go back to yesterday, but so much of what we think is valid today is whether we 'connect' to it. There's nothing wrong about that, of course, but so often what we 'connect' to is what has a link with our past. Some call it our 'comfort zone'. If it reminds us of where we've been, we are more likely to accept it. If someone we trust says something new we will take it on board every time, but if we don't like the person we tend to be suspicious no matter how valid his or her point may be.

I once listened to a friend of mine read aloud a statement that gripped him. I replied, 'I like that – read it again.' He did. 'Who said that?' I asked. When he told me my stomach churned. I began to see what I could find that was *wrong* with what was said. It was by a person whose views on so many issues are those I reject categorically. Then I realised how childish I was being. Either I will recognise truth for its own sake or I am going to embrace the thoughts only of those who adhere to my way of thinking. I felt convicted to my fingertips. I vowed then and there to be a seeker of truth, no matter who says it. Paul said, 'I am bound both to Greeks and non-Greeks, both to the wise and the foolish' (Rom. 1:14). If Paul can express a debt to the foolish, surely I can accept truth, even if it is stated by my enemy!

Joseph Tson once asked me, 'How far are you willing to go in your commitment to Christ?' We must be willing to follow truth no matter where it leads us. This is the only way you and I can recognise and experience today's anointing.

One of the paradoxes of church history is that the anointing has been characterised by both continuity and discontinuity. By continuity I mean what continues unchanging. For example, the Gospel. That does not change. It continues from age to age. By continuity I also mean that there is a scarlet thread that runs from Genesis to Revelation, showing the blood of Jesus in every age and on every page. It began with the first promise of redemption, 'And I will put enmity between you and the woman, and between your offspring and hers; he will crush your head, and you will strike his heel' (Gen. 3:15). It was first demonstrated in the Garden of Eden after the Fall: 'The LORD God made garments of skin for

Adam and his wife and clothed them' (Gen. 3:21). It was evident in Abel's offering when he brought 'fat portions from some of the firstborn of his flock' (Gen. 4:4). That scarlet thread was unveiled in the Law by the ancient sacrificial system. That continuity continues to the present day, for the message is that Christ died for sinners, shed his precious blood. 'Salvation is found in no one else, for there is no other name under heaven given to men by which we must be saved' (Acts 4:12).

Continuity. 'Jesus Christ is the same yesterday and today and for ever' (Heb. 13:8). This tremendous statement was placed in the context of the warning: 'Remember your leaders, who spoke the word of God to you. Consider the outcome of their way of life and imitate their faith' (Heb. 13:7). For there is absolute continuity with the message. So Jude began his brief epistle: 'Dear friends, although I was very eager to write to you about the salvation we share, I felt I had to write and urge you to contend for the faith once delivered to the saints' (Jude 3). This message must never change. It was the message of Athanasius, the message of Augustine, the message of the Reformers, the message of Wesley and Whitefield. Continuity. Today's anointing will have an unbroken continuity with the past, linking with that scarlet thread.

By discontinuity I mean the manifestation of God's anointing that may have no obvious precedent. It may appear and disappear. That it had no precedent does not invalidate its authenticity. That it may not last long does not mean it wasn't right at the time. An example of this is the strange phenomenon in the early Church when all the believers 'had everything in common. Selling their possessions and goods, they gave to anyone as he had need' (Acts 2:44–5). Many of us find this very odd. It didn't last. But the seal of God on this practice became apparent when Ananias and Sapphira acted as though they were in on it but lied. God struck both of them dead in the space of three hours (Acts 5:1–10). There is no biblical principle that states that Christians are to do what the early Church did for a time. But there is equally no doubt that this is what happened for a while. I am sure it seemed natural to those who did it at the time. Discontinuity.

Not long ago I led my church to adopt a prayer covenant that includes four petitions, which we pray literally every day. The third petition is this: 'We pray for the manifestation of the glory of God in our midst *along with an ever-increasing openness in us* to the manner in which you choose to manifest that glory.' Why this? First, the only manifestation we care about is the manifestation of the Lord's glory. We want nothing else. But I also saw that God might not choose to manifest his glory precisely as he did yesterday. I'd be happy if he did. I could live with the 'glory' I saw in the early Nazarenes. I could live with what I believe to be true about the Welsh Revival of 1904–5. But God may or may not accommodate us with what coheres with our comfort zone. Hence we pray as much for ourselves to be *open* to God's sovereign choice as to how he may wish to manifest his glory, as we do for that unveiling itself.

Four days after we had the new prayer covenant cards printed up, my friends Lyndon Bowring and Charlie Colchester joined me for an evening in London's West End. Just before we went to see *Schindler's List* we went to a Chinese restaurant in Gerrard Street. While waiting for our food, Charlie spoke up: 'Have you guys heard about this Toronto thing?' Neither of us had a clue what he was talking about. He began to describe how at his church, Holy Trinity Brompton, people were being prayed for after the service and then falling to the floor in laughter. Lyndon and I looked at each other, rolled our eyes heavenward, and listened as Charlie was clearly gripped by what had been happening. He asked, 'Do you think this could be of God?' I replied that if you put me under a lie detector I would say it was *not* of God. We finished our meal and went to the cinema, but I found myself thinking of that conversation even more than the unforgettable film we saw.

I unveiled our new prayer covenant publicly the following Sunday. When I explained the implications of the third petition – the prayer for the manifestation of God's glory and our being open to the manner in which he chose to manifest that glory – I referred to the Toronto phenomenon. I stated that I did not believe it was of God *but* that one must always be open to unusual things like this, since church history has taught us God *can* surprise us with the unusual and unprecedented. In any case I had gone on public record that this particular phenomenon was not of God.

A few days later a ministers' meeting was being held on the Chapel premises. Lyndon Bowring introduced me to Bob Cheesman, who had recently returned from Toronto. Bob's face was beaming. His life had been dramatically changed, he said. I invited him to come to the vestry and pray for me. I was unconvinced but still felt I had to be open. In the meantime a close friend had turned up to have coffee with me in my vestry. I explained to him that I had just invited a man recently returned from Toronto to pray for me. 'You've heard about Toronto,' I assumed. He hadn't. I quickly explained what I knew about it. He is a fellow minister of reformed views who was about as interested in what I had just described as I might be in toe dancing on ice. Seconds later there was a knock on the door, and Bob came in. The two ministers already knew each other and obviously had mutual respect for each other. I explained that Bob was going to pray for me and that the other man could look on. 'He can pray for me too,' my friend said courteously. As we stood to pray there was another knock on the door – Gerald Coates had come to say hello. I said, 'Bob is just getting ready to pray for me.' Gerald replied, 'I want in on this.' So now four of us were praying. They were praying for me. But, as best I can recall, not ten seconds had elapsed when my friend fell forward – right on the floor of my vestry, face down. I gulped and swallowed hard. 'I am impressed, I must admit.' I said nervously. Ten minutes later the *three* of them commenced praying for me. Nothing happened. But that was the moment I was forced to reassess my opinion.

Not long after, Ken Costa, churchwarden at Holy Trinity Brompton, phoned. 'Something unusual has happened at our church and I was wondering if you have written anything on 1 John 4:1–4' – a passage that discusses testing the spirits and distinguishing false prophets from true. He sent a courier immediately to fetch tapes of four sermons I had preached from that passage. He took me to lunch soon afterwards to discuss what was going on at HTB. By the time lunch was over I knew in my heart I had been on the wrong side of something God was in. I could see myself in the succession of those who opposed Edwards, Whitefield, Wesley and the Welsh Revival. I said to my wife Louise after that lunch: 'I am going to have to climb down.' I shared the same with my deacons that Friday evening.

The following Sunday, just before my morning prayer, I made a public climb-down on Toronto. 'How many times have you heard me say over the years, "What if revival broke out at All Souls, Langham Place, or Kensington Temple? Would we be willing to affirm it even though it wasn't here at Westminster Chapel?" ' (Mind you, I never thought I'd have to do that.) On that morning I affirmed that God was at work at HTB and we prayed publicly for Sandy Millar, their vicar and my friend.

My fear from that day on was twofold. First, I was afraid that this move of the Spirit would not come to Westminster Chapel. Second, I was afraid that it *would* come to Westminster Chapel. But I was determined to do nothing that would make it happen. For a great while I did not know if it ever would come to us. Our people generally were not prepared for anything like what was happening in churches like HTB or

Queen's Road, Wimbledon. We could cope with the familiar or the nostalgic or what played into our comfort zone. This was too different. A stigma too great.

Many of us are very happy if God is so kind as to 'do it again' like he's done it before. In this we are happy. For this we are quite ready. Moreover, there is little stigma here. Almost none. We want to avoid any stigma when it is outside our comfort zone. 'What will *they* think? What will they say?' Today's anointing is *totally missed* by looking over our shoulders, probably more than by any other factor.

In early 1905 an English couple living in India arrived in Southampton, returning home for one reason: to see the Welsh Revival. They came up to London and ran into old friends whom they trusted.

'What are you doing back home?' their friends asked.

'We heard that revival has broken out in Wales, and we wouldn't miss it for anything.'

'It is nothing but Welsh emotionalism,' their friends replied.

Believing that, the couple boarded a ship heading for India and missed seeing the move of the Spirit in Wales entirely. That move of the Spirit, largely singing with little preaching, was not like previous revivals.

Discontinuity. This is what threatens us. When there is no precedent that we can put our finger on. The precedent for the unprecedented, however, is biblical. It is the theme running right through Hebrews 11, the faith chapter of the Bible. Not a single person mentioned there had the luxury of repeating yesterday's anointing. Enoch walked with God (Gen. 5:24). Noah walked with God (Gen. 6:10). There was the continuity. For all I know, Noah grew up hearing about the legendary Enoch, who walked with God, 'then he was no more, because God took him away' (Gen. 5:24). So we are told, 'By faith Enoch was taken from this life, so that he did not experience death; he could not be found, because God had taken him away. For before he was taken, he was commended as one who pleased God' (Heb. 11:5). Noah therefore did what Enoch did – he walked with God. The continuity of a comfort zone may have made Noah feel that what happened with Enoch would happen to him. But no. One day God said,

> So make for yourself an ark of cypress wood; make rooms in it and coat it with pitch inside and out. This is how you are to build it: The ark is to be 450 feet long, 75 feet wide and 45 feet high. Make a roof for it and finish the ark to within 18 inches of the top. Put a door in the side of the ark and make lower, middle and upper decks. I am going to bring floodwaters on the earth to destroy all life under the heavens, every creature that has the breath of life . . . will perish. But I will establish my covenant with you, and you will enter the ark – you and your sons and your wife and your sons' wives with you. (Gen. 6:14–18)

Noah's critics might have said, 'There's no precedent for making an ark – you are a fool and you most certainly aren't hearing from God.' It wasn't easy for Noah. But he set the precedent for God's glorious but painful discontinuity: 'By faith Noah, when warned about things not yet seen, in holy fear built an ark to save his family. By his faith he condemned the world and became heir of the righteousness that comes by faith' (Heb. 11:7). It had never happened before and it never happened again.

Abraham might have said, 'Perhaps God will lead me to build an ark.' But God did not require that of Abraham. There was something more difficult than building an ark. 'By faith Abraham, when called to go to a place he would later receive as his inheritance, obeyed and went, even though he did not know where he was going' (Heb. 11:8). Not knowing where we are going, yet knowing we are following God, can be most painful indeed. God has a way of giving us sufficient revelation for ourselves but not enough that it convinces others.

The stigma is knowing you have heard from God but having to do what no one else may be required to do. Jesus told Peter how he would die. 'I tell you the truth, when you were younger you dressed yourself and went where you wanted; but when you are old you will stretch out your hands, and someone else will dress you and lead you where you do not want to go' (John 21:18). Peter sadly could only think of John: 'What about him?' (John 21:21). The stigma of solitude doubles the pain. If only *one other person* could join me – or see what has been revealed to me!

Dr Lloyd-Jones used to say to me, 'The Bible was not given to replace direct and immediate revelation from God; it was given to correct abuses.' There is not the slightest hint in the New Testament that the Bible, once completed, would replace God's supernatural dealings with us. Some good people hold to the 'cessationist' view of scripture, that the miraculous (signs, wonders, prophecy, direct guidance) ceased when the canon of scripture was completed. This is held by some to explain why there seemed to be less and less of the miraculous in church history. It was a neat view that enabled people not to worry if the extraordinary revelation from God, whether through prophecy, word of knowledge or in people being miraculously healed, did not occur. It was assumed that God himself decreed this; now that we have the Bible we do not need the direct witness.

This would mean that God could not talk to us today as he did, say, to Philip. An angel of the Lord said to him, 'Go south . . .' Later the Spirit said, 'Go to that chariot and stay near it' (Acts 8:26,29). Consequently we would not have such intimacy with God today as to be 'kept by the Holy Spirit from preaching the word in the province of Asia' (Acts 16:6). Or having a vision that said, 'Come over to Macedonia, and help us' (Acts 16:9). Or having an angel stand beside us to say, 'Do not be afraid' (Acts 27:24). It is supposed that our knowledge of the Bible should be so complete and sufficient that we are above needing such revelation.

Really? We need it as much as ever. There is nothing more comforting – or scary – than knowing that God can speak to us in a clear and direct manner. There is equally nothing so comforting as seeing that it is what happened in the Bible. And yet we have what the early Church didn't have – the New Testament to keep us on the straight and narrow. If there is any word of knowledge or prophetic insight that *conflicts* with scripture, we stay with *scripture* and reject the word of knowledge – no matter who gave it. The scriptures do not replace the miraculous; they correct abuses when people hear 'words' that *couldn't* have come from God because they don't cohere with biblical theology.

But the anointing will often offend. That is not surprising, for it stretches us. It brings together both the continuity and the discontinuity of God's dealings with us – the God of the past and the Lord who acts in the 'now'. Such majesty and mystery are rarely within our comfort zone.

8

Moving outside our Comfort Zone

Samuel was ordered to move outside his comfort zone. 'The LORD said to Samuel, "How long will you mourn for Saul, since I have rejected him as king over Israel? Fill your horn with oil and be on your way; I am sending you to Jesse of Bethlehem. I have chosen one of his sons to be king"' (1 Sam. 16:1). When God says, 'How long will you mourn?' the implication is that Samuel has been in that state for a good while. And too long. But after a while, even though we are mourning, we can get used to it – and begin to live with it. Even to like it. What was once upsetting can become comfortable. We get used to it. This is why some people coming out of prison, which they hated at first, want to return.

I remember when a filling came out of a tooth. It left a big hole and I had a panicky feeling about it. I intended to go to a dentist immediately, but because the pain was only marginal I kept putting it off. I got used to the big hole in the tooth. But a few months later I had to go to the dentist for another reason. The dentist spotted the big hole and said he would take care of it while I was there. 'Oh, no,' I said. Then, feeling embarrassed that I had said that, I kept quiet as he filled the hole. I really missed that hole. I loved sticking my tongue down in it. It became a comfort zone.

It is like the Leaning Tower of Pisa in Italy. Were it not for the historic tower there most of us would never have heard of Pisa. But a few years ago it was discovered that the tower was, although very slowly, beginning to lean too much. The city fathers had an emergency meeting – what were they to do? There was only one thing to do: bring in architects and professional builders who would ensure that the tower did not topple over. But this injunction came to the professionals: keep the tower from falling over but don't correct the tilt! In other words, make sure it stays like it is.

We are all like that. We want to stay as we are. After many years of pastoral experience I think perhaps I have learned at least one thing: people don't want their problems solved, they want them understood. But I decided on one occasion to help solve a lady's problem. She would come into my vestry virtually every single week with the same essential problem. I asked her: 'Do you want your problem solved or merely understood?'

'Oh, I want it solved – please help me.'

I did. That is, I tried. I told her what her problem was, and what she might do. She sent me a note the following week saying that the Lord was leading her to another church! I never saw her again.

I know some Christians who love to mourn. Not just moan. Mourn. Mourn for sin. Really! They love it. They love preaching that makes them feel awful and unworthy. They love preaching that gets close to the bone. They love to feel, 'I am no Christian after hearing this word.' It is not that they *really* feel they are not Christians, it is only that they love being chastised by 'close' preaching. They never intend to change, mind you. They love feeling uncomfortable – it is a comfort zone.

I went to hear a rather well-known reformed preacher whose text was Luke 6:46: 'Why do you call me, "Lord, Lord," and do not do what I say?' I never heard anything quite like it.

He applied the text from soteriology (the doctrine of salvation) to ecclesiology (the doctrine of the Church), with marriage and the family thrown in between. He even said, 'If your wife doesn't think of Jesus when she sees you – since you are to love her as Christ loved the Church – how can you say you are a Christian? You call Jesus, "Lord," but do not do the things he said.' Well. That certainly put me in *my* place. And yet a friend actually said to me afterwards, 'Wasn't that wonderful?' I replied, 'I will ask you one thing. If what he said is *really* true, how can *you* now be sure *you're* a Christian?' Never mind, that didn't matter to my friend; the main thing was that it made one feel so awful! But there are people like that. A miserable feeling is right in the middle of their comfort zone.

An old friend of mine spent an hour telling me how Arthur Blessitt rebuked Southern Baptists for not witnessing enough. This was when the Southern Baptist Convention was being held in Los Angeles. They invited Arthur to leave His Place (described below) long enough to address some thirty thousand Southern Baptists. My friend told me that Arthur really went for them.

'What difference will thirty thousand Southern Baptists make in Los Angeles after your coming here?' Arthur reportedly said.

'It was terrific,' my friend said. 'I never heard anything like it in my life.'

But when I brought Arthur to London and decided to do in Westminster what Arthur hoped for in those Southern Baptists, my old friend dropped me like a hot potato. He loved it when he was challenged to witness – in Los Angeles. But not at home. He loved being miserable – up to a point. But to get him outside his comfort zone? Not a chance.

God told Samuel to stop mourning for what could not be helped and to start looking for tomorrow's man. This would take courage. And Samuel would do it alone.

At the end of the day the anointing will have a stigma. It will offend. John Wesley was offended by George Whitefield going to the fields to preach since it wasn't in a regular church building and it hadn't been done before. But John Wesley eventually went to the fields too. Wesley also criticised Whitefield because of the unusual manifestations that characterised Whitefield's preaching – people falling down on the ground, laughing, shaking, some barking like dogs. Wesley rebuked Whitefield for allowing this and urged that, at least, Whitefield deal with what was patently of the flesh if not the devil. Whitefield replied that if you try to stamp out the wildfire and remove what is false you will equally and simultaneously remove what is real. One has to let things be, said Whitefield. Wesley eventually acquiesced and subsequently witnessed the same mixture of manifestations in his own ministry too, and agreed to let things be.

Our comfort zone is usually not too disturbed if there is a good precedent for what is happening. We equally like to think that when God is at work there will be no evidence of the counterfeit. Or false professions of faith when the preaching is over. When Billy Graham preached in Westminster Chapel over eighty people came forward during his gentle appeal. One man was high profile; his name is in the papers from time to time. We never saw him again, and this would include most of those who came forward. But not all. Some were genuinely converted. Most of those who pray to receive Christ during our Pilot Light Saturday morning witnessing on the streets we never see again. But not all are like that. Some are genuinely converted. Am I to believe such a ministry is not of God because of the counterfeit professions? No. Part of the stigma is that we cannot present a neat package to our fearful friends and prove God's manifestation. We have to go with the flow of God's general move and let the stigma remain a stigma.

I had no idea of ever being a witness on the streets. I was

always glad for somebody else to do that. I figured I'd 'paid my dues' by being faithful to the Gospel in my Sunday preaching. I admired those who did 'personal work', as it has been called. I looked up to those who gave tracts to people on the Tube, witnessed to a waiter or waitress in a restaurant or talked to a stranger on the train. But that wasn't my anointing!

All that kind of reasoning changed. It started when I invited Arthur Blessitt to preach at Westminster Chapel during May 1982. That in itself took its toll. Some of my best supporters were absolutely indignant that I invited Arthur to my pulpit. 'He's all right for Speakers' Corner,' some said. But was I to believe that if a John the Baptist or an Elijah came to town I couldn't have him in a church that (rightly or wrongly) regarded itself as a citadel of British evangelicalism? 'Whatever have we come to?' I wondered. But fire was in my bones. All the king's horses and all the king's men would not stop me from inviting this man to preach for me.

Arthur Blessitt had built a twelve-foot wooden cross and put it up on a wall in his coffee house, called His Place, in Hollywood's Sunset Strip in the 1960s. One day God told him to take it down and carry it around the world. People thought he was crazy. But he did it. He carried that cross all across America, Canada, Europe, Great Britain, Africa and the Middle East – and by now almost every country on the globe. He witnessed to every Israeli general, stayed in Prime Minister Begin's home, spent a day witnessing to Yasser Arafat, was awarded the Sinai Peace Medal, has been sought after by heads of state. But he was unwelcome by some at Westminster Chapel because of his style. He wore jeans.

He turned us upside down. After two weeks with us he said, 'We must get out on the streets.' I thought, 'Oh, no.' I asked him to address our young people one Friday night. The idea was, after he finished, we'd take our pamphlets and questionnaires to nearby Page Street – the only street where we could successfully knock on doors. As we headed out for Page Street after Arthur's compelling address, Arthur saw three young people standing at the zebra crossing in front of the Chapel. I took his arm to lead him to Page Street but Arthur wouldn't go with me – he began talking to these three young people. I kept looking at my watch as he talked on and on. But – guess what? Two of them wanted to be saved. They prayed to receive the Lord. I kept looking at my watch. But Arthur pulled out another tract, his follow-up pamphlet which showed (1) what has just happened to you and (2) what to do now (pray, read your Bible every day . . .). I thought he'd never finish. When he did I said, 'Arthur, we need to get to Page Street.' He ignored me as he saw another young man standing right in front of Westminster Chapel. In twenty minutes that man was on his knees in tears.

Arthur turned to me. 'Dr Kendall, I don't know where this Page Street is, but you don't need to leave the steps of your church. The whole world passes by here.' I was never to be the same again. In that moment I had what I'd call a vision. I saw a pilot light, like in a cooker or oven, which stays lit day and night. I said to Arthur, 'Why couldn't we have coffee available here on the porch of the Chapel and have a ministry talking to passers-by right here?' In that moment the Pilot Light ministry was born. I never looked back.

But the cost was terrific. All I had preached consistently and faithfully for the previous five years suddenly came under attack. The invitations to preach (I was getting an average of one invitation to preach somewhere in Britain every day) came to a halt. Ministerial friends distanced themselves from me. Members of the Chapel began resigning their membership right and left. 'This is simply not Westminster,' the people would say to me. Those were hard days. But I have never been sorry I invited Arthur and walked in the light God was giving me then. If you ask me, it was my finest hour.

I now doubt I would have survived had I not obeyed the

Lord in those days. I have little doubt that God would have taken his hand off me and replaced me with someone who would listen. And yet it wasn't easy. It hurt my pride. It isn't fun to have some of your best supporters tiptoe away from you because your obedience embarrasses them. It is part of the stigma.

New challenges were to emerge further down the road. It was years before we enjoyed again the unity we had before 1982. When we finally achieved it, I decided I'd never again do anything controversial. I figured I'd done enough to show I would obey God. I wanted to live out my days in Westminster Chapel in peace but hoping, of course, revival would come without my having to stick out my neck again! To quote a phrase I used above, 'I'd paid my dues.' No more risks for me.

Until I met Paul Cain. When I first heard of Paul, as I said in the beginning, I honestly felt he was occultic. The incredible accuracy of his words of knowledge – calling people out by name and giving their birthdays and addresses or their personal details – sounded to me an awful lot like what the devil does. Isn't it interesting how we are so ready to ascribe the miraculous to Satan? Wyn Lewis asked whether I would like to meet Paul. Yes, although I was not prepared that such a man could really have a gift like Samuel or Elisha. But I changed my mind when I met him. After four hours with him I felt humbled to think that I could be his friend. I said I'd never do it again, after the trouble caused by Arthur Blessitt's visit, but I asked Paul to preach for us. A new era began again. But the stigma was greater than ever. More loss of support. More cancellations.

There is more. In December 1994 Colin Dye asked me if I'd like to meet Rodney Howard-Browne. Yes. I knew that the Toronto phenomenon was traceable to Rodney – the falling down, the laughter. But I was expecting no more than to meet him. As soon as I met him I sensed that across the breakfast table was a guileless man of God. 'Baby Isaac,' I kept thinking, 'Baby Isaac.' In October 1992 Paul Cain and I had held the first Word and Spirit conference at Wembley. Graham Kendrick wrote a hymn for us, 'Jesus, restore to us again', which demonstrated the need for the word and the Spirit to come together. I preached a sermon that amounted to a prophetic statement: as Abraham sincerely believed that Ishmael was the promised child, so have many assumed that the charismatic renewal *was* the revival the Church had been praying for. Wrong, I said. Isaac is coming. What God is going to do ahead will be a hundred times greater than anything the Church has yet seen. It will be as proportionately greater as the promise contained in Isaac was greater than that which pertained to Ishmael. It offended charismatics because they felt I was calling all of them Ishmael; it offended evangelicals partly because I affirmed the charismatic renewal as something God was in (for there was a place for Ishmael in God's sovereign plan).

I knew little about Rodney Howard-Browne. All I know is, 'Baby Isaac' kept coming to me as I looked at him across the breakfast table. I also remembered a word Paul Cain gave to our deacons in March 1993: 'Isaac will be an ugly baby. He will look like Ishmael, he will burp like Ishmael, he will have to have nappies changed like Ishmael. But as an ugly baby sometimes turns out to be a beautiful person, so Isaac will be the most handsome person ever.' Baby Isaac. Isaac means 'laughter'. I did not know then that Rodney himself had always seen his own ministry as unstopping wells – the only thing Isaac ever really did (see Genesis 26:18–32). Rodney's main verse – which he quotes nearly every time he preaches – is John 7:38: 'Out of his belly shall flow rivers of living water' (AV). I did not know this either. But I now know that the thrust of his ministry, giving joy and laughter by the laying on of hands, he bases on John 7:38. The origin of the joy and laughter is from within a person. Rodney's ministry is to unstop the well, so that the joy will flow.

I hadn't heard Rodney preach but I asked him if he would be prepared to stop by my church the following Saturday morning. Why? I wanted him to stand in my pulpit and pray (I had done the same thing with Paul Cain), then I wanted him to pray for my wife Louise. He arrived the next Saturday, went up to the pulpit and prayed aloud in the empty auditorium. We returned to the vestry for him to pray for my wife.

Louise had been in a severe depression for five years or more. At one stage it was so awful that I thought I'd have to give up my ministry and return to America. Parallel with the depression she developed a bad cough. Her GP sent her to the Royal Brompton Hospital, and we feared the worst. The cough became so severe that often she could not sleep a night through without having to get up for a couple of hours. She also developed an eye condition, seeing flashing lights in her peripheral vision, and was advised to go to the casualty department at St Thomas's Hospital. The consultant warned her that the cough could result in a detached retina.

Rodney and his wife Adonica prayed for Louise for about five minutes. She was instantly healed. That was in December 1994. In January 1995 she spent a week at Rodney's meetings in Lakeland, Florida. 'It's the nearest you get to Heaven without dying,' she said to me on the phone from Lakeland. She returned to London transformed. Our son T R got in on this and his life too was turned upside down.

Our son T R (Robert Tillman II – we call him T R) was living in the Florida Keys when Louise went over to Lakeland. He had planned only to take her to his home but came a day early at her insistence. He was not the slightest bit interested in the sort of thing Rodney emphasised, but agreed to stay just for an hour or two. Before the evening was over he was taken up by a ministry he had never seen before. A month later he went to New Orleans to hear Rodney and was touched by the Spirit in a very, very powerful way. Two months later he accepted an offer to work for one of our deacons, Benjamin Chan, a computer programmer, so he returned to London.

In the meantime he began watching videos of Rodney's ministry and got some of our young people interested in them. That October T R took a group of our young people to hear Rodney. The following Sunday night, after the close of the regular service, I asked those who had heard Rodney to give their testimony. Not all were touched in the same way but when they finished giving their testimonies I turned to the congregation and asked: 'How many of you would be interested, if the opportunity were given, to be prayed for by these young people, along with our deacons?' Hands went up all over the congregation. Well over half the people came forward to be prayed for! That was the night 'Toronto' made its way into Westminster Chapel. I was thrilled to bits but also scared out of my wits.

In December 1995 I invited Rodney to preach in Westminster Chapel. It was an unforgettable evening. People one would never dream would be touched were on the floor laughing their heads off, having been prayed for by Rodney. Lives were changed. But some were upset. In thirty days or so we had twenty resignations. Our church treasurer warned me early in 1996 that the giving would be off by 15 per cent. That was a good bit of money. But by the end of 1996 we were 4 per cent up over the previous year.

Revival has not come to our church despite all the risks I have had to take. But our unity is the best I have known it, our finances better than at any time in our history. God has taken us through every single crisis. He will for you, too – anyone who is willing to endure the stigma.

As for 'Baby Isaac', time will determine the rightness of that impression. But if pressed, I believe the Church throughout the world is in the embryonic phase of the greatest work of the Spirit this century. It *has* been an ugly baby. The falling down, the laughing and other manifestations are not always a pretty sight. Rodney Howard-Browne prayed for Randy Clark whose hands were 'frozen' when he was prayed for. 'Lay hands on anything that moves,' Rodney said to Randy. Soon after, Randy was preaching at the Airport Vineyard Church in Toronto. A powerful anointing – and stigma – was deposited on John Arnott's church. Soon they came there from all over the world to be prayed for. The *Daily Telegraph* nicknamed the new phenomenon 'The Toronto Blessing'. It has spread to England, Europe, South Africa, Australia, Scandinavia, the Third World and to Pensacola.

The stigma. Why is it that so many sovereign vessels put people off? Arthur Blessitt by his unconventional style. Paul Cain by his prophetic ministry. Rodney by his laying hands on people. It seems that every generation has its stigma by which the believer's faith is tested. But why must some of the best, most knowledgeable and most refined of God's people be put off? Can't they see genuine men of God? I have had to come to terms with the fact that the best of Christians sincerely get put off by the anointing. I only wish that the anointing could come in a neat and tidy package that plays into our comfort zone. It rarely does.

9

Today's Man or Woman

Samuel is a type of today's servant of Christ on the lookout for tomorrow's servant. 'So God said to Samuel, "How long will you mourn for Saul, since I have rejected him as king over Israel? Fill your horn with oil and be on your way; I am sending you to Jesse of Bethlehem. I have chosen one of his sons to be king" ' (1 Sam. 16:1).

Samuel was now on the spot. He had to break with yesterday's man, Saul, whom he had discovered and put in power, and at the same time find and anoint tomorrow's man, David. In seeking tomorrow's man Samuel was at considerable risk. Samuel said to the Lord, 'How can I go? Saul will hear about it and kill me' (1 Sam. 16:2).

I sometimes wonder which is more painful: being yesterday's man or woman, today's man or woman or tomorrow's man or woman. Yesterday's man endures the pain of irrelevance, having known what it was to be used of God. And yet if he *thinks* he is still under the same anointing he once had, he still suffers by knowing in his heart of hearts he is struggling with great effort to convince himself and others he is still on the cutting edge of what God is doing today.

The pain of being tomorrow's man or woman is that you have to wait – sometimes much longer than you thought. The preparation is hard, God having to mould and shape you for your usefulness at the proper time. 'How long, O Lord?' you cry as David did (Ps. 13:1). We are never quite prepared for the rigid disciplining God puts us through for the calling he has destined us for.

The pain of being today's man or woman largely comes from the degree of courage required with the job. We never feel up to it. 'Who is equal to such a task?' (2 Cor. 2:16). We may well feel like Gideon. The Lord addressed him as a 'mighty warrior' (Judg. 6:12). His response: 'How can I save Israel? My clan is the weakest in Manasseh, and I am the least in my family' (Judg. 6:15). Gideon still needed the 'fleece' to be wet, then dry, before he could carry on (Judg. 6:36–40). He felt anything but a mighty warrior. Moses too felt unprepared. 'Moses said to the LORD, "O Lord, I have never been eloquent, neither in the past nor since you have spoken to your servant. I am slow of speech and tongue" ' (Exod. 4:10).

It took courage for Samuel to pronounce King Saul as yesterday's man, *because* Saul continued to wear the crown. Samuel was therefore nervous about going to the house of Jesse to anoint the next king since the present king was very much alive.

God seems to love putting today's servant in the most awkward situations. Joseph, who was engaged to Mary, had to make the hard decision to marry her, when she was pregnant by the Holy Spirit, knowing what people would think of the two of them for the rest of their lives (cf. John 6:42). It required a vision before Joseph decided to marry her. God told Abraham to sacrifice Isaac, the only link between himself and the promise of a seed that was to be as vast as the sand of the sea – and only one step at a time at that: sacrifice him on 'one of the mountains I *will tell you about*' (Gen. 22:2). Elijah was promised that he would drink from a brook at Kerith, only to find, 'Some time later the brook *dried up* because there had been no rain in the land' (1 Kgs. 17:7).

And yet by the time Samuel had to break with the regime of which he had been no small part, he was highly seasoned and trained in the knowledge of hearing God's immediate voice. His initial training came early. It too required having to break with one regarded as today's man but who was rapidly becoming yesterday's man – Eli the priest. Samuel was very young at the time. He looked up to Eli with uncritical adulation and respect. Eli could do no wrong, Eli alone heard from God. So when the Lord called, 'Samuel!' Samuel immediately went to Eli and said, 'Here I am; you called me,' a scenario that was repeated three times. Finally Eli twigged what was happening – that God was actually calling directly to the young Samuel. It is to Eli's everlasting credit that he recognised that God was at work. 'So Eli told Samuel, "Go and lie down, and if he calls you, say, 'Speak, LORD, for your servant is listening."' So Samuel went and lay down in his place' (1 Sam. 3:9).

Samuel was getting a kind of training every servant of Christ must undergo: seeing that those we have admired aren't perfect. Eli was highly respected in Israel at the time and the young Samuel would have stood in awe of him. It was hard for Samuel to accept that God would speak directly and immediately to him and not through the revered Eli. But Eli had a blind spot – he tolerated his sons in their mishandling of the things of God. And yet Eli knew the Lord and had a heart after God. The deaths of his sons, clearly a judgment of God, no doubt grieved him. But what grieved him *more* was the mention that the ark of God was taken from Israel, which led to his own death (1 Sam. 4:18).

No saint of God is perfect. As Solomon said in his prayer at the dedication of the temple, 'There is no one who does not sin' (2 Chron. 6:36). Eli had his blind spot; we all have them. Calvin even said that in every saint there is something reprehensible. And yet we all like to think that our own heroes are perfect.

My father was a great admirer of preachers. He frequently invited them into our home for meals, particularly visiting evangelists and conference speakers who would come to our church. I would listen intently to every conversation, hanging on to every word. If my dad admired preachers, I did even more. They were my heroes.

But I began to discern as I grew older that these men had imperfections and weaknesses. I tended to sweep such under the carpet in my mind, but eventually I came to terms with the fact that the best of men are men at best.

Until my new hero came along. I remember saying to him over thirty years ago, calling him by name, 'You know, every person I have ever begun to admire too much sooner or later disappointed me – but I know that *you* never will.' I actually said that. I have to say that within a few months of that naïve testimonial, the man I so admired became the source of my greatest disappointment and severest trial up to then. It happened when I preached things that made him uneasy. His friends had accepted me but became disillusioned with me because they could see that he was not going to uphold what I was teaching. He and those friends deserted me in my dark hour. It took years and years before I recovered.

We do our admirers no favour to let them adulate us or get too attached to us. We are going to disappoint them – it is only a matter of time. I will say frankly and candidly that it scares me nearly to death when I discern that someone, especially a new Christian, is regarding me as their hero. I know they will crash when they know how vulnerable and human I really am.

Samuel, therefore, being distanced from Eli by God's own intervention, was being trained for a much more difficult test that he would face years later – having to call a spade a spade regarding the very man he discovered: Saul.

God was in the process of preparing today's man. 'And the LORD said to Samuel: "See, I am about to do something in Israel that will make the ears of everyone who hears of it tingle" ' (1 Sam. 3:11). From that moment God and Samuel had an unbroken intimacy.

> The LORD was with Samuel as he grew up, and he let none of his words fall to the ground. And all Israel from Dan to Beersheba recognised that Samuel was attested as a prophet of the LORD. The LORD continued to appear at Shiloh, and there he revealed himself to Samuel through his word. And Samuel's word came to all Israel. (1 Sam. 3:19–21)

It must have been hard for Samuel to accept himself as God's man for today. He assumed Eli was that. Every person God uses in the here and now sooner or later must discover God for themselves. Second-hand revelation no longer will do. We must learn to recognise God's voice so clearly and distinctly that we know we aren't being deceived. But it is sobering and humbling.

How do we recognise God's voice? Like young Samuel, we aren't always sure at first what is going on. It is good when a veteran – like Eli – can help us. But the older generation won't always be around. The torch will be passed to us, unworthy though we feel and are.

A few years ago I came up with an acrostic – P.E.A.C.E. – which has been helpful for me. Generally speaking, this has served me well. It is a *general* way of knowing God's will and whether or not we have truly heard God's voice. I put the following questions:

P – is it providential? If God gives a word, it will cohere with his providence. In other words, does God open the door or do we have to knock it down? If I have to pry a door open it is a fairly good hint I am in the flesh. Providence refers to God's way of governing: his overruling, his going before us, his way of arranging circumstances – the 'coincidences'. If it is providential – that is, if a door is open without your having to open it yourself – move on a bit and look for other tests.

Samuel was ordered to go to the house of Jesse. But would Jesse accept him?

Samuel was welcomed by Jesse. Jesse had several sons. So far, so good. There was nothing unprovidential about Samuel's visit to Jesse. Had Jesse not welcomed Samuel, the great seer would have had to say, 'I've got it wrong.' If Jesse had had no sons, only daughters, Samuel would have had to climb down and admit God had not sent him.

An ambitious, 'spiritual' man went to Charles Spurgeon with a word from the Lord. 'The Lord told me to preach for you tonight,' said the man to Spurgeon. But Spurgeon replied, 'Sorry, but the Lord hasn't told me that.'

In my Trevecca days I thought the Lord told me I would marry a beautiful blonde girl. Nothing was clearer to me. But not a single blonde-haired lady would even give me the time of day. I ended up marrying a lovely brunette – God's real choice for me. Imagine how far I would have got had I said to every blonde, 'The Lord told me I would marry you.' What worries me now is that I could have held to the idea of the blonde – and missed Louise! But I suspect there are not a few sincere Christians who fancy they have heard from God and won't accept advice from friends.

When God is at work, doors open. His providence is a good hint that you are not being deceived. It isn't the only test, but I would say it is an essential ingredient in knowing whether you have heard from God. If it is providential, move on and put another question.

E – the enemy: what would he want you to do? Your enemy is the devil. He comes as a roaring lion (1 Pet. 5:8); he masquerades as an angel of light (2 Cor. 11:14). The roaring lion comes to intimidate. The 'roar' is to make you say, 'I'm finished,' so you will give in and let him destroy you. The angel of light comes to deceive, so you will think you are hearing from God – or that you are in the presence of a man or woman of God – when it is a complete deception.

When I was a student at Trevecca I worked in the summer for the government in Washington, D.C. A person I trusted put me in touch with an unusual man. I was very taken with him, and he had me eating out of the palm of his hand in a short period of time. He based everything on the Bible. He had charts of the books of Revelation and Daniel that explained *everything* – from the seven trumpets to the seven vials of God's wrath. He said it was revealed to him that he was one of the two witnesses of Revelation chapter 11; he was Elijah. The other was Moses, 'somewhere in Europe'. He told me I was special. I liked that. He also said that the Second Coming was to be on 11 October 1957. As to Jesus' words, 'You know neither the day nor the hour', a *few* were allowed to be in on the secret. He was a complete fraud and I am happy to say I discovered this prior to October 1957. God rescued me and it taught me a lesson. Had I not been set free I might have been destroyed.

When we are given an impression, impulse or feeling that we think could be of God, we should ask, 'What do we suppose the devil would want us to do?' In other words, most of us have a fairly shrewd idea what the devil *hopes* we will do with a certain feeling. *Do the opposite* and you will be right most of the time. This is relevant with regard to sexual temptation, intellectual temptation, financial temptation, social temptation or temptation connected with ambition. If you will calmly figure out in your mind what your enemy the devil hopes you will do in a given situation and then do the opposite, you will almost certainly be safe from years of regret. But there is more.

A – Authority: the Bible What does God's word say? The Holy Spirit will never, never, never lead us to do anything contrary to God's revealed will – the Bible. 'How can a young man keep his way pure? By living according to your word' (Ps. 119:9). 'I have hidden your word in my heart that I might not sin against you' (Ps. 119:11). 'Do good to your servant, and I will live; I will obey your word' (Ps. 119:17).

The Holy Spirit wrote the Bible, using consecrated men and women (2 Tim. 3:16; 2 Pet. 1:21). He will not lead us in a way that does not cohere with holy scripture. However strong the impulse, however powerful the feeling, however clear the vision, do not listen to or obey any 'word' that doesn't affirm God's word.

I knew of a married man who fell in love (he called it that) with a married woman. His wife didn't understand him or desire him any more, her husband didn't understand her or desire her any more. But they met each other, understood each other and desired each other. This is why the first point, providence, isn't enough to know you are hearing from God. But they felt they heard from God, so what they decided to do – sleep with each other – met with God's approval 'in this particular case'. What does the Bible say?

> It is God's will that you should be sanctified: that you should avoid sexual immorality; that each of you should learn to control his own body in a way that is holy and honourable, not in passionate lust like the heathen, who do not know God; and that in this matter no one should wrong his brother or take advantage of him. The Lord will punish men for all such sins, as we have already told you and warned you. For God did not call us to be impure, but to live a holy life'. (1 Thess. 4:3–7)

Sin and temptation are always 'providential'. Jonah said 'No' to God's command to go to Nineveh and decided to go to Tarshish instead. Lo and behold, when he went to the dock there was a ship ready to sail for Tarshish (Jonah 1:3)! It made him feel confirmed in what he had already decided to do. Providence, then, is not enough.

The Holy Spirit will always affirm the Bible. He will always lead us in a way that dignifies the plain teaching of scripture. If your 'word' from the Lord goes against the teaching of God's word, you did not hear from God after all.

C – confidence Does the impression you have received increase or diminish your confidence? Be honest here. Does the thought of obeying this 'word' increase your confidence? If so, that is a good sign. If you lose confidence, it is a bad sign.

I find that when I am pleasing the Lord my confidence is at a fairly high level. When I lose confidence it does *not* mean I am seriously out of God's will; after all, if our hearts condemn us, 'God is greater than our hearts' (1 John 3:20). He gives more grace (James 4:6). And I know what it is to feel a lack of confidence and have God nonetheless affirm me. But I wouldn't want to make a major decision at a time like that! It is better when our hearts do not condemn us and we have confidence before God (1 John 3:21).

When I hear a word, get an impulse, feel an impression to do something, I ask myself: how do I really feel? I have learned that a lack of confidence is a warning signal not to proceed.

But this can be tricky. The fear of man can get in and cause us to miss a wonderful, wonderful blessing. I therefore have to ask: why am I afraid? 'Who is going to harm you if you are eager to do good?' (1 Peter 3:13). When I can see that my lack of confidence is based upon the fear of what people might think, I ask: what does God think? If a great sense of confidence swells up inside I have learned to recognise it as a warm, sure signal that I am hearing from God.

Confidence, boldness, assurance and inner liberty were what enabled Peter to preach on the Day of Pentecost (Acts 2:14–36). It is the Greek word *parresia*, translated 'confidently' (Acts 2:29), 'courage' (Acts 4:13), 'bold' (2 Cor. 3:12), 'confidence'

(Heb. 4:16). When that comes, especially if combined with the other four points in the acrostic, I am quite sure I am not being deceived. The final test, if all the above suggest a green light, now follows.

E– ease: what you feel in your heart of hearts It is when you are being true to yourself. Conscience. What you feel deep down inside when you are being true to yourself. God will never lead you to be untrue to yourself. He will never lead you in such a way that you violate your conscience.

This alone – ease – is not enough. It must follow the four previous propositions, if you choose to accept my acrostic. If *all five* don't fit, I would say that God is not speaking to you. If all five fit it is a good sign – not an infallible sign, since it is but a general hint – that you are not being deceived.

P.E.A.C.E. 'Let us therefore make every effort to do what leads to peace and to mutual edification' (Rom. 14:19). When we do the things that make for peace we will *feel* peace and *make* peace.

At the end of the day peace has governed me more than anything else in making decisions, big and small. One of the fruits of the Spirit is 'peace' (Gal. 5:22). It is deep and very powerful. 'You will keep in perfect peace him whose mind is steadfast, because he trusts in you' (Isa. 26:3). I cannot recall a single major decision I have ever made that I later came to regret when it was preceded by that peace. But I can recall decisions I made which I later regretted when I proceeded without that peace. The lack of peace is like a flashing red light that says 'Stop!'

Even the small decisions – like accepting an invitation, whether to meet someone, what sermon to preach, what article to write. That peace is a test – whether you will obey when you've got it, and whether you will obey by saying 'No' when you haven't got it. I remember a friend asking if he could give a particular preacher my phone number. There was no peace. I said, 'No.'

'What? Nobody refuses a chance to meet this man!' said my friend.

But a few months later I discovered why I had no peace and could see that God was sparing me a lot of needless embarrassment.

Today's man or woman must develop a network, or code, or channel – call it what you will – by which they *know* they recognise that voice. The aforementioned acrostic is a beginning. But eventually one needs an even more refined instrument through which God speaks clearly. You probably (1) won't be allowed to tell anyone how you know, and (2) couldn't convince them anyway. God wants a special relationship with you – just you – by which you know you are not being deceived when he speaks. God 'confides' in those who fear him (Ps. 25:14).

Samuel had that. God let none of his words 'fall to the ground' (1 Sam. 3:19), contrary to my experience years ago when I thought I would marry a blonde. I've had to learn many lessons the hard way. It may take time to develop an intimacy and godly familiarity by which you and I can know God's voice. But it is worth waiting for and crucial to the anointing for being today's man or woman.

> So he asked Jesse, 'Are these all the sons you have?' 'There is still the youngest,' Jesse answered, 'but he is tending the sheep.' Samuel said, 'Send for him; we will not sit down until he arrives.' So he sent and had him brought in. He was ruddy, with a fine appearance and handsome features. Then the LORD said, 'Rise and anoint him; he is the one.' (1 Sam. 16:11–12)

Samuel had no peace until he saw young David. But when he saw David he recognised the voice that had never let him down. 'Then the LORD said, "Rise and anoint him; he is the one" ' (1 Sam. 16:12).

Today's man or woman recognises God's voice – the very thing the Hebrew Christians were in danger of losing (Heb. 5:11). The real issue is recognising the Spirit. A good question to ask, then, is how long does it take to recognise the Holy Spirit? The sooner, the better. Everybody eventually will see the truth. Today's servant of Christ must learn to see it early on.

IO

The Loneliness of Anointing

> Fill your horn with oil and be on your way; I am sending
> *you* to Jesse of Bethlehem. (1 Sam. 16:1)

No one else – you, Samuel.

Samuel might have said, 'Why me?' As far as I know, he
didn't. But many of us have done so. Moses did. Having been
given his commission to confront Pharaoh, Moses said, 'O
Lord, please send someone else to do it!' This did not make
God very happy; the Lord's anger 'burned against Moses'
(Exod. 4:13–14).

In earlier days Samuel had the opposite problem; he had to
learn not to take rejection personally. Every leader has to
learn this. In Samuel's case it came when Israel demanded a
king. Samuel knew this was wrong. He warned them on
bended knee. He was distressed. 'And the LORD told him:
"Listen to all that the people are saying to you; it is not you
they have rejected, but they have rejected me as their king" '
(1 Sam. 8:7).

When we take rejection personally we will need a lot more
of God's fiery disciplining. It's hard not to take rejection
personally, especially if you have been close to the people
who can't go along with you. God graciously assured Samuel:

they haven't rejected you but me. When we know we are carrying out God's mandate we have an authority that withstands the most vehement criticism. We become humbly conscious that God has deemed to elevate us to the Big League – and we follow in the path of those lonely leaders who heard from God.

A few years ago I found myself gripped by John's words in Revelation 1:9: 'I, John, your *brother and companion* in the suffering and kingdom and patient endurance that are ours in Jesus'. I was going through a major trial at the time. Those words seemed to beckon me to *move up higher* in my relationship with God. It was as though John were speaking to me. I felt John's loneliness. I was lonely. I felt that God was saying, 'Welcome to the Big League' – a realm known by those willing to suffer. I thought too of those words, 'We must go through many hardships [much tribulation – AV] to enter the kingdom of God' (Acts 14:22).

Loneliness. It goes with the job of being today's man or woman. We live in a day when collective leadership is in vogue. The greater the consensus, the lighter the stigma. This way we can pass the buck to each other.

It does not follow that we should not listen to others. We must be accountable. We all need those around us who will not be rubber stamps and who will warn and rebuke. 'As iron sharpens iron, so one man sharpens another' (Prov. 27:17). Those who remain unteachable and unaccountable because they have achieved a measure of success will almost certainly be found out and lose credibility – if not their anointing – at the end of the day. 'Wounds from a friend can be trusted' (Prov. 27:6). Fallen leaders can be partly explained by an absence of their being accountable to others.

On the other hand, today's man often walks alone. Samuel did. Moses did. Abraham did. Elijah did. Paul did.

Samuel now had to break with the regime he had set up. He had to turn away from what God did yesterday. Although

Samuel had initially opposed the idea of kingship, he went along with it because God told him to. Once he came to terms with God's fresh word – 'Let them have a king' – Samuel gave all his energy to it. To use a colloquial expression, the kingship and the discovery of Saul to wear the crown was Samuel's baby. He actually became the architect of the whole thing. But now he was told to abandon it. The same God who had accommodated Israel with a king now regarded Saul as finished.

It wasn't easy to do this. First, accepting the kingship. Second, abandoning it. Both were the result of obedience to God's fresh revelation. From one point of view Samuel could be seen as being vacillating. Was he for Saul or not? The truth is, Samuel was taking orders from God.

The paramount stigma of being today's man or woman is probably that of being misunderstood. Nothing is more painful than this. We can cope with a lot that people say against us – as long as they are fully in the picture and still disagree. But what *hurts* is when they *aren't* in the picture and form judgments and perceptions that are based on limited information.

I sometimes think that much of Jesus' pain at the crucifixion was through his being misunderstood. Nothing made sense. It didn't add up that the same man who raised Lazarus from the dead a few days before was now hanging on a cross. Why didn't Jesus *stop* the proceedings that led to the crucifixion? Anybody who could control the wind and storm on the Sea of Galilee could surely have intervened before Herod or Pilate. When a detachment of soldiers fell back (John 18:6) Jesus could have fled. There were any number of ways in which he could have stopped being crucified. Common sense told everybody this. So why was he being crucified? The disciples couldn't figure it out – they all forsook him and fled (Matt. 26:56). Never once did Jesus explain himself. It must have been almost unbearable emotional pain for Jesus to see Mary Magdalene sobbing her heart out at the scene of the cross and not be allowed to whisper to her, 'It's OK, Mary, all is going according to plan, I'm atoning for the sins of the world by my blood.' But there was no hint of this. He had to bear the further stigma of being misunderstood, even by those closest to him.

Only Samuel knew that Saul was yesterday's man. He had to make a decision: should he stick to his guns by supporting Saul right or wrong, or listen to that voice which had never failed him yet? He listened to God.

This serves to show how all relationships must ever be subservient to God's greater glory. No matter how close people get to each other they must be closer to God. The irony is, the closer people are to God, the more they will love each other. The more they put the voice of God prior to their commitment to each other, the more they really respect each other.

I think of some of my close friends. The dynamic that holds us together is that we love God more than we do each other. If I stopped listening to God and turned away from him I would expect my friends to warn me – then lovingly rebuke me if I did not come to my senses. It works both ways. If my closest friend broke with the principles that spawned our relationship, however much he has been like a brother, I would warn him and rebuke him – but I would keep loving him. No friendship or relationship is worth its salt if it does not have an inflexible commitment to God's glory first and to one another second. It would break my heart if I had to break with any of my friends – for any reason. But I would do it if I had to because of my greater love for God's honour.

That is what Samuel had to do with Saul. Today's man is often in the awkward position of having to do this. One must put any sentimental attachment to one side. Nostalgia has to go. The precious memories would never be sufficient to keep a relationship intact if all were not *equally* committed to hearing God's voice.

Have you ever had to do this? Have you had to say farewell to a person, a church, an organisation or group of friends with whom you had been in sweet company? It was not because *you* got off the rails – they did. You would have been loyal to the end. But they broke faith. Perhaps you felt betrayed. 'Even my close friend, whom I trusted, he who shared my bread, has lifted up his heel against me' (Ps. 41:9). No covenant with any person, church, group or organisation should be based on sheer human loyalty to one another. It is love for God that brought about the fellowship in the first place.

It is a severe test to one's mettle whether God will always be put first – and obeyed. Today's man or woman must get his or her approval from God only. 'How can you believe if you accept praise from one another, yet make no effort to obtain the praise that comes from the only God?' (John 5:44). It is a way today's servant of Christ must bear the cross. But the more I bear this cross, the more I put God's voice first, the more I am jealous of God's glory the more will I be respected, appreciated and loved by these friends. That in fact is what makes real friendship.

If you wish to be today's servant then you must also resist gloating when you have been vindicated. If Samuel had been small-minded he would have been glad Saul had failed the test. Samuel was the only one who warned against the kingship. We therefore might expect him to shout to the housetops, 'I told you so.' How do we know he didn't do that? Because God said to Samuel, 'How long will you *mourn* for Saul, since I have rejected him as king over Israel?' (1 Sam. 16:1). There was no gloating, only mourning. 'Do not gloat when your enemy falls; when he stumbles, do not let your heart rejoice' (Prov. 24:17).

A good evidence that you and I can be trusted with today's anointing and today's stigma is that we mourn when a brother or sister slips or falls. Cain said, 'Am I my brother's keeper?' (Gen. 4:9). The answer is yes. I fear that the anointing many of us desire is largely delayed because of a rival spirit. We look over our shoulders and, consciously or unconsciously, compete with one another. Virtually no consideration at all is given to seeking the glory that comes only from God. We want mutual adulation more.

D L Moody sat on the platform and heard the speaker say, 'The world has yet to see what God could do with one man totally resigned to him.' What that man meant was this: someone who wants *only* God's honour, not man's, someone who has no grudge against a soul and who doesn't care what people think as long as one follows the Holy Spirit. Internally, D L Moody said, 'I propose to be that person.' It changed Moody's life and Moody began to change the world. But not without considerable suffering in the meantime.

Today's man or woman ought also to be on the lookout for tomorrow's man. 'The LORD said to Samuel, "How long will you mourn for Saul, since I have rejected him as king over Israel? Fill your horn with oil and be on your way; I am sending you to Jesse of Bethlehem. I have chosen one of his sons to be king" ' (1 Sam. 16:1). As long as our deep concern is for the status of tomorrow's generation we are in fairly good shape.

Perhaps the saddest moment in Hezekiah's life was when Isaiah warned him that he ought never to have allowed certain Babylonians to gaze on the things in the palace at Jerusalem. Isaiah prophesied,

> Hear the word of the LORD: The time will surely come when everything in your palace, and all that your fathers have stored up until this day, will be carried off to Babylon. Nothing will be left, says the LORD. And some of your descendants, your own flesh and blood, that will be born to you, will be taken away, and they will become eunuchs in the palace of the king of Babylon. (2 Kgs. 20:16–18)

This ought to have sobered Hezekiah through and through. Instead, his only comment? '"The word of the LORD you have spoken is good," Hezekiah replied. For he thought, "Will there not be peace and security in my lifetime?" ' (2 Kgs. 20:19). He was not thinking of the next generation but only of himself.

Jonathan Edwards said that the one thing Satan cannot successfully counterfeit is a love for the glory of God. As long as you and I truly love God's honour, including the reputation of *his* Church today and tomorrow, it is good evidence we haven't been duped by the devil. But if it is my own reputation I worry most about, there is no proof I am today's man. Quite the opposite.

Samuel, one of the greatest men that ever was, simply followed the Lord all his days, no matter how he appeared to men. He was a symbol of today's servant of God. He was on the lookout for tomorrow's man.

Samuel assumed that the next king of Israel would be Jesse's first-born. Samuel saw Eliab and thought, 'Surely the LORD's anointed stands here before the LORD' (1 Sam. 16:6). Any servant of Christ has his biases. Samuel knew that the first-born of any family would receive double the inheritance. But God had broken that pattern before. Isaac, not Ishmael, was God's anointed. Jacob, not Esau, was God's anointed. So it was about to happen again. The Lord said to Samuel, 'Do not consider his appearance or his height, for I have rejected him. The LORD does not look at the things man looks at. Man looks at the outward appearance, but the LORD looks at the heart' (1 Sam. 16:7).

Samuel began to think he had missed the Lord's signal. Jesse had first brought Eliab, then Abinadab, then Shammuah. All Samuel could say was, 'Nor has the LORD chosen this one' (1 Sam. 16:9). Jesse had seven of his sons pass before Samuel. He still could not feel right. 'The LORD has not chosen these' (1 Sam. 16:10). Today's servant of Christ must be willing to hear the voice of the Spirit above his own personal biases and prejudices. So Samuel asked Jesse, 'Are these all the sons you have?' (1 Sam. 16:11).

Had Samuel followed his instinct he would have gone by 'outward appearances'. He must have thought this when he saw Eliab and he said to himself, 'Surely the LORD's anointed stands here before the LORD.' But that is when God's voice transcended Samuel's instinct.

It is not always easy to tell the difference between our instincts, shaped by years of knowledge and experience, and the voice of the Spirit. This is where many of us fail. We hastily go by outward appearances – our comfort zone.

I sometimes think that God picks people whose natural style is quite off-putting. Like Arthur Blessitt with his cross, wearing jeans in the pulpit at Westminster Chapel. Or George Whitefield's squint. His critics called him 'Dr Squintum'. They said of the Apostle Paul, 'In person he is unimpressive' (2 Cor. 10:10). As for John the Baptist, 'John's clothes were made of camel's hair, and he had a leather belt round his waist. His food was locusts and wild honey' (Matt. 3:4). That was apparently odd even then. Uncle Buddy Robinson, an early Nazarene evangelist, left school at the age of nine, was tongue-tied and would have been rejected by any seminary. But he won over 250,000 souls to Christ in his day. Rodney Howard-Browne has been known to put off some who seem sophisticated but he has an anointing that defies a natural explanation.

I equally wonder if God sets up a stigma that is so off-putting that people can feel at home in their disgust. For example, we may feel a certain person's manner or message is disgusting. When we react so violently inside we instinctively feel right to be so indignant. It seems so right to feel this way that we are quite at home in our annoyance. But I have found that many times my deep negative reaction was not only wrong, it was a test from God to see if I would look again –

and see why I was so upset. I have learned again and again that I have been on the verge of *rejecting* the very anointing I was later glad I embraced.

Have you learned to recognise God's set-up? This is what we find in John 6. The moment Jesus' words began to offend – 'I am the bread that came down from heaven' – the crowds drew on information they had always known: 'They said, "Is this not Jesus . . . whose father and mother we know? How can he now say, 'I came down from heaven?' " ' (John 6:42). The offence in some people's anointing is camouflaged by God's set-up. This way people can rationalise and dismiss the person and feel completely justified. When Jesus went so far as to say, 'Unless you can eat the flesh of the Son of Man and drink his blood, you have no life in you' (John 6:53), that did it. 'This is a hard teaching. Who can accept it?' (John 6:60). 'From this time many of his disciples turned back and no longer followed him' (John 6:66). They could not have felt more justified in their disgust. But God set them up.

Eliab, Jesse's first-born, was a set-up. 'This is surely the one,' even Samuel thought at first. But fortunately Samuel kept listening to that voice he trusted.

> So he asked Jesse, 'Are these all the sons you have?' 'There is still the youngest,' Jesse answered, 'but he is tending the sheep.' Samuel said, 'Send for him; we will not sit down until he arrives.' So he sent and had him brought in. He was ruddy, with a fine appearance and handsome features. Then the Lord said, 'Rise and anoint him; he is the one.' (1 Sam. 16:11–12)

It was as though Jesse said, 'There is one more son but you surely won't want him.' Many of us, like the couple who missed seeing the Welsh Revival, are put off by well-meaning, sincere people. But Samuel said, 'Send for him; we will not sit down until he arrives' (1 Sam. 16:11).

One of the most famous sights in Kentucky is Mammoth Cave, the largest underground cavern in the world. We used to think it was one of the Seven Wonders of the World (what the other six were I never knew), and it is worth seeing. Many tourists go there but when they come close there are signs everywhere describing other caves in the area. They are given all sorts of names, and the hype to get the tourists to stop includes signs such as 'The most beautiful cave in the world'. Some people stop and go into these and never see Mammoth Cave.

If we are not truly tuned into the voice of the Holy Spirit we can let any prejudice of our own charm us to miss the authentic. On top of this God may well test us by allowing our prejudice to overrule when someone's outward appearance is not up to what we think should befit an anointed servant of Christ.

Once Samuel saw David, despite his young age and utter lack of experience, the Lord said, 'Rise and anoint him; he is the one' (1 Sam. 16:12). How did Samuel know? I only know that he knew. He knew he was not deceived. But he would not have been able to supply evidence to Jesse or anyone else that would be totally convincing. The pain of being today's man is that you can't convince another person of what you see unless the same Holy Spirit shows them as well.

I would like to say a further word about my own father. He wasn't perfect and yet I think he was the godliest man I have ever known. His prayer life possibly had more to do with influencing me than any other factor. I repeat, he was not a church leader or minister. He was a layman. And yet he prayed thirty minutes every day. I doubt there are many laymen like him in the world today, and I feel so fortunate to have had a father like I had.

My greatest sorrow therefore was that my dad was utterly unconvinced of my new revelations (a new theology, knowledge that God would use me one day). I came home from

Trevecca during the era I was having my most intimate communion with God. I not only had visions but would get an immediate impression to open my Bible to a verse – voiced within by the Spirit – that I did not know. When my father showed his keenest displeasure one day – which shook me rigid – I felt an impression to turn to Philippians 1:12, having no idea what it was. But that verse, which held me in the days that followed, read: 'But I would ye should understand, that the things which happened unto me have fallen out rather unto the furtherance of the gospel' (AV). Without knowing it I had embraced teaching that my old denomination found deeply offensive. I knew that I was eternally saved after 31 October 1955. God showed me predestination and election in the Bible. I was given a great sense of sin and unworthiness and yet my life was spotless. Nobody around me was impressed. My dad was horrified. But I knew that what was revealed was absolutely true. I have not wavered in over forty years. And yet I have not been able to come up with any neat framework to convince another person – my dad or closest friend – that what is revealed to me is of God. I only wish there were such a formula; it would save a lot of deep hurt and embarrassment.

Today's servant of Christ must therefore put his or her personal wishes – even relationships – to one side. It is a lonely road. 'Who is equal to such a task?' I have had to watch members of my churches over the years see their closest friends go in opposite directions. It hurts to witness this. Closest friends. Brothers and sisters. Parents and sons and daughters.

Do not suppose that I have come to bring peace to the earth. I did not come to bring peace, but a sword. For I have come to turn

'a man against his father,
a daughter against her mother,

    a daughter-in-law against her mother-in-law –
    a man's enemies will be the members of his own
    household.'

Anyone who loves his father or mother more than me is not worthy of me; anyone who loves his son or daughter more than me is not worthy of me; and anyone who does not take his cross and follow me is not worthy of me. Whoever finds his life will lose it, and whoever loses his life for my sake will find it. (Matt. 10:34–9)

My first public test – that is, outside my sphere of family and old friends – was when we moved from Fort Lauderdale to Carlisle, Ohio. I was recommended to preach by one who at the time was my closest friend and mentor. I preached two sermons and they called me to be their pastor. I anticipated no problems down the road because they said they had no doctrine or creed: 'No book but the Bible, no creed but Christ, no law but love.' That sounded good to me. But when I preached the Bible it was against their 'creed of tradition' and they showed little love. Not all, however. Some believed what I preached. In doing so I watched closest friendships disintegrate before my eyes. Those who opposed my teaching and preaching got up a petition to get rid of me. My old friend and mentor utterly rejected me. I left after eighteen months, returned to Florida to sell vacuum cleaners. The trauma of the era lasted for years. But it prepared me for battles far greater than anything I experienced then. 'He that is faithful in that which is least is faithful also in much' (Luke 16:10 AV). God gives little tests – however great they seem at the time – to get us ready for the battle royal.

Part of the sacrifice of being today's servant of Christ is that vindication usually comes tomorrow. Possibly after we are in heaven. Partly what made those in Hebrews 11 'today's' servant in their day was that they were willing to have the fruits of their labours borne by a successive generation. 'These were all commended for their faith, yet none of them received what had been promised. God had planned something better for us so that only together with us would they be made perfect' (Heb. 11:39–40).

Peter reminded his readers that, as for the prophets of the Old Testament, 'It was revealed to them that they were not serving themselves but you, when they spoke of the things that have now been told you by those who have preached the gospel to you by the Holy Spirit sent from heaven. Even angels long to look into these things' (1 Pet. 1:12).

This is an example when those *with the Lord* continue to be today's men and women. I would dare say that if one never becomes yesterday's man or woman in one's lifetime that person could always be relevant in some way. 'God is not unjust; he will not forget your work and the love you have shown him as you have helped his people and continue to help them' (Heb. 6:10). Those Hebrew Christians who did not succumb to the pressures of their day would never be forgotten.

Paul Cain sometimes says, 'I am too old to disobey God.' I think I know what he means by that. Not that you reach an age when you are incapable of disobedience, but that you see time running out and you know it isn't worth it to be influenced by any voice but the Holy Spirit. 'We must all appear before the judgment seat of Christ' (2 Cor. 5:10). I have had increasingly to make every decision, preach every sermon and write every word as if I were summoned at any moment to stand before God. I am too old now to count on a second chance to get things right.

Samuel wanted to leave not a personal legacy by which he would be remembered, but a legacy for Israel tomorrow. That is what made him today's man. Had he thought of himself he would have been perilously close to becoming yesterday's man.

We all are guilty of thinking of ourselves and how we will

be remembered. But the irony of church history is that those who prepared most for tomorrow's Church were the most remembered; those who wanted to build their own empires became yesterday's men and women while they were still alive – and hardly remembered afterwards.

When he was president, Ronald Reagan kept a little plaque on his desk that read, 'There is no limit to how far one can go as long as he doesn't care who gets the credit.' That to me is profound. If you and I can bring that into our own lives I suspect it would make a considerable difference – not only in our usefulness but in how we are remembered. It would mean wanting, first of all, the honour that comes from God only, then to affirm his servants, no matter who they are. That is the challenge of being today's man or woman.

Steve Chalke, preacher and TV personality, has an anointing 'to tell the world about Jesus', as he puts it. He is prepared to do this any way he can. God has highly gifted Steve, who has a creative mind beyond so many of us who admire him. What is the secret to this anointing? I think I discerned it in a conversation in which he unwittingly revealed that secret. It happens that Steve has presented to the powers that be an imaginative plan for the millennium, that is, what might be done to celebrate coming into the year 2000. The idea, absolutely brilliant, would show the way forward by which the enormous debts of the Third World countries could be cancelled. It was a remarkable solution, and this was apparently appreciated by those to whom it was presented. There was one problem, however. Certain men at the top struggled as to who precisely would get the credit for it. 'I don't care who gets the credit for it,' replied Steve, 'I just want it to happen.' But there is more: all this would give honour to One who paid our debt two thousand years ago. My point is this. When one truly does not care who gets the credit for any brilliant idea, but just wants to see it carried out, there is no limit to how far that person can go.

TOMORROW'S ANOINTING

The Secret Anointing

Tomorrow's servant of Christ is typified by David. He had the anointing without the crown. Yesterday's man – Saul – had the crown but not the anointing. He remained king but was rejected in God's sight. 'So Samuel took the horn of oil and anointed him in the presence of his brothers, and from that day on the Spirit of the LORD came upon David in power' (1 Sam. 16:13).

David's anointing was a secret anointing. Only ten people knew about David's anointing: Samuel, Jesse (David's father), David's seven brothers and David himself. A highly dangerous ritual had taken place: Samuel had anointed Israel's next king while the present king was alive and well. Nobody else was to know of this for many years.

It was an anointing that David had not sought. He had been tending the sheep when, out of the blue, he was summoned to be anointed king over Israel. Not unlike Joseph, who unexpectedly was summoned to appear before Pharaoh (Gen. 41:14). God has a way of finding us when his time has come.

The event must have been overwhelming for the young David. But he had been earmarked by God who saw David as a man after his own heart (1 Sam. 13:14). David had developed certain gifts and talents that would stand him in good stead soon after his secret anointing: musicianship and bravery – an unlikely combination. As a rule a musician is cerebral and emotional, scholarly if not rather delicate. The rugged athlete – a 'man's man' who is the 'outdoorsman' and at home in the wild – is normally not the type one expects of an accomplished musician. But David was both.

Despite his age his reputation preceded him. When Saul's attendants needed someone who could play the harp to drive an evil spirit from tormenting the king, someone thought of David. 'One of the servants answered, "I have seen a son of Jesse of Bethlehem who knows how to play the harp. He is a brave man and a warrior. He speaks well and is a fine-looking man. And the LORD is with him" ' (1 Sam. 16:18). With nothing of course, being known about the anointing on David that would prepare him for his ultimate calling, he was brought to play for King Saul who immediately liked him very much. 'Whenever the spirit from God came upon Saul, David would take his harp and play. Then relief would come to Saul; he would feel better, and the evil spirit would leave him' (1 Sam. 16:23).

This was David's first opportunity to perform in the royal service. His musicianship was blessed by the Holy Spirit. Little did he know that he would one day transform worship in Israel, write psalms that would become a vital part of scripture or that he would become known as the sweet singer of Israel (2 Sam. 23:1, cf. AV).

David's next opportunity that demonstrated his secret anointing was facing Goliath. The secret anointing goes from strength to strength. Playing the harp before Saul was a small test. As we have seen, he that is faithful in that which is least is faithful also in much (Luke 16:10), and the 'much' was next on God's agenda for David. It is what would give David a high profile in Israel but would mean only a step towards further preparation.

We may think that the 'much' that follows the 'least' means we have arrived. But the 'much' may lead us to an era of long preparation that is designed for the secret anointing entrusted to us. Any anointing needs to be refined. The young David wasn't yet fit to be king, but God was about to give him a wide profile among the people of God that would precipitate the next stage in David's preparation.

There are several kinds of preparation. There is academic preparation. Sadly, some seem to think this is the most important. It may not be unimportant but it is not the most important. God has chosen some men and women for works of service who had little if any academic preparation – the great Charles Spurgeon, for example. It is an embarrassment to this present day that Regent's Park College, then in London but now in Oxford, rejected the young Spurgeon for admission![1] The Methodist Church turned down G Campbell Morgan as a candidate for the ministry; he was regarded as unsuitable! He later became minister of Westminster Chapel and gave it an international reputation.

The most important kind of preparation in any case is spiritual preparation. It is what refines and develops the spirit. It is what prepares the way for usefulness in God's hands. It is not an easy kind of preparation. It is when we find out what people are like, how mean and unkind they can be – those closest to us and those often thought to be the most spiritual. It is when we also learn our own hearts aren't perfect.

God raised up David to become Israel's greatest king, but he also raised him up to receive the spiritual refinement that would make him a true man of God. It would be hard to say whether God raised up David for Goliath or God raised up Goliath for David – to show what he could do in that which is 'much' – to get David ready for the long haul ahead.

Israel was running scared because of the giant Goliath – over nine feet tall – who challenged Israel to pick a man who would fight him.

Goliath stood and shouted to the ranks of Israel, 'Why do

you come out and line up for battle? Am I not a Philistine, and are you not the servants of Saul? Choose a man and have him come down to me. If he is able to fight and kill me, we will become your subjects; but if I overcome him and kill him, you will become our subjects and serve us.' Then the Philistine said, 'This day I defy the ranks of Israel! Give me a man and let us fight each other.' On hearing the Philistine's words, Saul and all the Israelites were dismayed and terrified. (1 Sam. 17:8–11)

In the meantime King Saul had promised three things to the man who would kill Goliath: great wealth, the king's daughter in marriage and exempting his father's family from paying taxes (1 Sam. 17:25). David's response was simple: 'Who is this uncircumcised Philistine that he should defy the armies of the living God?' (1 Sam. 17:26). David's secret anointing enabled him to see the enemy for what he was before an omnipotent God. The secret anointing enables one to see what others can't see or are afraid to say.

David volunteered. 'David said to Saul, "Let no one lose heart on account of this Philistine; your servant will go and fight him" ' (1 Sam. 17:32). The secret anointing showed David what he knew he could do. David therefore could see what the others couldn't see, say what others were afraid to say and volunteer to do what no other person would do.

Do you have a secret anointing? You are conscious that God is with you. You are given discernment. Courage. Motivation. It is not that your time has come in terms of what God will ultimately do for you, but you have been handed an opportunity on a silver platter which you cannot refuse. This was the way David felt.

But nobody believed David. 'Saul replied, "You are not able to go out against this Philistine and fight him; you are only a boy, and he has been a fighting man from his youth" ' (1 Sam. 17:33). At this point David recalled earlier experiences that showed he had been prepared for such a time as this. As David was a musician before he was employed in the royal service so also had he become at home in the wild. What David had been given by common grace, as we saw earlier, was now under a new anointing. And yet David knew what he had done before this secret anointing had come on him.

> But David said to Saul, 'Your servant has been keeping his father's sheep. When a lion or a bear came and carried off a sheep from the flock, I went after it, struck it and rescued the sheep from its mouth. When it turned on me, I seized it by its hair, struck it and killed it. Your servant has killed both the lion and the bear; this uncircumcised Philistine will be like one of them, because he has defied the armies of the living God. The Lord who delivered me from the paw of the lion and the paw of the bear will deliver me from the hand of this Philistine.' Saul said to David, 'Go, and the LORD be with you.' (1 Sam. 17:34–7)

Another test emerged. David had to be true to himself and, in a word, be himself. Having been adorned with a coat of armour and a bronze helmet together with a sword over the tunic he was wearing, he knew in a flash that this would not do. ' "I cannot go in these," he said to Saul, "because I am not used to them." So he took them off' (1 Sam. 17:39). To quote Shakespeare again, 'To thine own self be true.' So David had to reckon with his true gift. It did not include fighting Goliath in Saul's armour.

One of the hardest types of preparation for one with a secret anointing is to accept his own ability and limitations. It took courage for David to reject Saul's kind offer of the traditional armour. But he knew in his heart that his way of defeating Goliath would have nothing to do with the heavy equipment Saul insisted on. 'Then he took his staff in his hand, chose five smooth stones from the stream, put them in the pouch of his shepherd's bag and, with his sling in his hand, approached the Philistine' (1 Sam. 17:40).

Goliath felt insulted when he saw the young David approaching him.

He looked David over and saw that he was only a boy, ruddy and handsome, and he despised him. He said to David, 'Am I a dog, that you come at me with sticks?' And the Philistine cursed David by his gods. 'Come here,' he said, 'and I'll give your flesh to the birds of the air and the beasts of the field!'

David said to the Philistine, 'You come against me with sword and spear and javelin, but I come against you in the name of the LORD Almighty, the God of the armies of Israel, whom you have defied. This day the LORD will hand you over to me, and I'll strike you down and cut off your head. Today I will give the carcasses of the Philistine army to the birds of the air and the beasts of the earth, and the whole world will know that there is a God in Israel. All those gathered here will know that it is not by sword or spear that the LORD saves; for the battle is the LORD's, and he will give all of you into our hands.' (1 Samuel 17:42–7)

David's secret anointing combined with his natural gift won the day. 'Reaching into his bag and taking out a stone, he slung it and struck the Philistine on the forehead. The stone sank into his forehead, and he fell face down on the ground' (1 Sam. 17:49). It was one of the most memorable moments in ancient Israeli history. It is summed up in one verse, which shows what God can do with one person with a secret anointing: 'So David triumphed over the Philistine with a sling and a stone; without a sword in his hand he struck down the Philistine and killed him' (1 Sam. 17:50).

But this was only the beginning of David's hardest era. Not that this victory was unappreciated. It was appreciated. King

Saul was very grateful. Furthermore, Saul's son Jonathan adopted David as his best friend (1 Sam. 18:2–3). David continued to grow from strength to strength, doing so well that the king gave him a high rank in the army. All was going so well for everybody concerned – until David got too much praise. When they were returning home, the women came from all over Israel to meet King Saul with singing and dancing, with joyful songs and with tambourines. By this time Saul may have thought within himself that the prophet Samuel had got it all wrong. 'The proof God is with me,' Saul may have thought, 'is that he sent David.' Until the women sang, 'Saul has slain his thousands, and David his tens of thousands' (1 Sam. 18:7).

Those accolades were – in a sense – the worst thing that could have happened to David. In that moment a breach emerged in his happy relationship with King Saul which meant that things between them would never be the same again. 'Saul was very angry; this refrain galled him. "They have credited David with tens of thousands," he thought, "but me with only thousands. What more can he get but the kingdom?" ' (1 Sam. 18:8). I do not know if Saul had those aforementioned thoughts about Samuel. He *had* to know that Samuel was displeased with him and that Samuel certainly believed Saul was finished. That Saul said, 'What more can he get but the kingdom?' indicates how insecure he was feeling. 'And from that time on Saul kept a jealous eye on David' (1 Sam. 18:9).

It has often been said that the greatest opposition to what God is doing today comes from those who were on the cutting edge of what God was doing yesterday, that the greatest hostility to what God is doing now comes from those who were on the front line of what God was doing yesterday. The greatest attacks on any current move of the Holy Spirit often come from those who were part of yesterday's move of the Spirit. The reason: jealousy.

From that moment David became a greater threat to Saul than the Philistines. David was a greater enemy than Goliath had been. David was a greater enemy than all of Israel's enemies combined. Saul directed all his attention and energy to one goal: eliminating David.

This is a scenario that has been repeated many times since – sadly, in the Church. It is when a rival spirit emerges among God's people and they get more intent on destroying each other than the real enemy in the world. But jealousy has a way of consuming us so that we convince ourselves that it is more important to get rid of our threat within than to see the lost won to Christ. Sometimes more literature comes off the press that attacks God's servants than anything else. If this were done by the secular press it might be a sign that we have at last annoyed the enemy outside. But it is unfortunately from Christians who hardly worry about the lost but occupy themselves with destroying a fellow-Christian's credibility. It is done to consolidate one's following and constituency – like Saul trying to save his own skin.

But there was a purpose in this. David wasn't ready to be king. God *might* have taken Saul away in his wrath then and there rather than wait for years and years. God had a different idea for David – that Saul be the means of David's sanctification! David wasn't ready to be king. He had a powerful anointing, yes. But he needed to be honed and refined. In the years to come, that anointing in David was to increase and develop so that when his time had truly come, David would be a transformed servant of the Holy Spirit.

A man or woman with a secret anointing always needs further preparation. It would be what would make David into a real man. A man's man he already was. But God knew there was a different kind of manhood needed. Paul said, 'When I was a child, I talked like a child, I thought like a child, I reasoned like a child. *When I became a man,* I put childish ways behind me' (1 Cor. 13:11). We do not get the necessary refinement by merely praying for more of the Holy Spirit. Jesus had all the Holy Spirit that there was – the Spirit without limit (John 3:34), yet, 'Although he was a son, he learned obedience from what he suffered' (Heb. 5:8).

I find this truly amazing. To think that Jesus, the God-man, needed suffering to be perfected. He was man *as though* he were not God – and was filled with the Spirit without any measure or limit set on that filling. He was *completely* filled with the Spirit. He was also God *as though* he were not man! And yet, 'In bringing many sons to glory, it was fitting that God, for whom and through whom everything exists, should make the author of their salvation perfect through suffering' (Heb. 2:10). All I can say is, if our Lord Jesus Christ needed to suffer before he could be all that God the Father envisaged for him, how much more do we – frail children of dust, and sinful (Jer. 17:9) – need to suffer before God can trust us with the full extent of the anointing?

Suffering was David's passport to a greater anointing. Though the Spirit came on him in power (1 Sam. 16:13), he needed Saul as insurance for yet more power. My grandmother used to say that the best way to live a long time was to get something wrong with you and take care of it! In a somewhat different way it seems that the best way to get closer to God is for God to give you a red-hot enemy – who is consumed with hatred for you – so that you learn what it is to become more like Jesus. King Saul's hatred of David was the best thing that ever happened to David. Little did David know that, rather than being crowned king in the next week or two, he would have years and years of fleeing Saul – for one reason: to guarantee that the secret anointing in him was refined.

But there was hope in it all. David got new energy from a new friend: Jonathan. Parallel with the suffering David was to experience in the ensuing years was a lifeline that gave him a little bit of joy. That lifeline to sanity and strength was also a pipeline into the royal house. David was able to know exactly what King Saul was feeling and what he was up to.

God knows how much we all need friends. A friend is someone who knows all about you and still likes you! If you and I have even just one friend like that, we are fortunate. David had the best. God will do this for you, too; your secret anointing will not only need refining but also a friendship that compensates for the suffering.

A true friend will tell you the truth. Some people only want friends who tell them what they want to hear; Somerset Maugham once said, 'When people ask you for criticism they really want praise.' They gather sycophants around them to bolster their egos. That is not a healthy friendship. David had in Jonathan not only loyalty but honesty. One of the most moving accounts in the life of David is when he and Jonathan made a covenant whereby Jonathan would tell David if indeed Saul was still out to get him (1 Sam. 24:16–17). David had to know the truth and he knew he'd get it from Jonathan. The result confirmed David's worst fears: Saul was determined to destroy him (1 Sam. 20:18–42).

David had already suffered a long time, running from Saul. But the result of David's covenant with Jonathan was to show David's real preparation for the kingship was not at an end but at the beginning.

In 1982 I was to undergo my greatest trial. As a result of having Arthur Blessitt in Westminster Chapel, some of my very best supporters and friends deserted me. I was feeling it keenly by the end of the year. But that was only the beginning. Throughout 1983 my opposition grew. By the end of 1983 the criticisms were beyond my wildest dreams. What I had preached, carefully and openly, since coming to the Chapel in 1977 was suddenly being attacked. Billy Graham preached for us in 1984, an event that could have helped most preachers, but by the end of that year six of our twelve deacons officially came out against me. A few days before Christmas I was served with a letter that would be sent to all the members of the church which described me as a heretic – I was accused of antinomianism (the view that says it doesn't matter how we live if we are saved). Our Christmas of 1984 was the bleakest we'd ever known.

The climax came at a church meeting on 16 January 1985. People turned up who hadn't been to church for ages but who were on the church roll. Those who had once been great supporters stood up and spoke against my teaching. My loyal supporters who were present were largely quiet. It was decided to take a break for a few minutes. I sat in solitude and silence. I had asked Jon Bush, my assistant, to be moderator. I turned and looked at Louise and T R who sat behind me. The look on Louise's face said, 'It's over – we're finished.' We'd be heading back to America and I'd return to selling vacuum cleaners. As I stared at the floor I heard a voice – from within: 'Don't lean on your understanding, trust in the Lord with all your heart.' It gave me peace. An unusual presence was at my right hand, almost at my fingertips. I will never forget that. The meeting reconvened and moments later the church overwhelmingly voted to dismiss the deacons who had falsely accused me. God brought us through and we have now served twenty-one years at Westminster Chapel.

I knew I wasn't an antinomian. As pastor I wanted, by God's grace, to produce a holy people. A number of those opposing me even said the same thing at the time. They sincerely felt that I was ruining the Chapel – by singing new songs and giving an appeal at the end of my sermons. One of the opposing deacons actually said to me that he didn't think I was antinomian but he disliked singing choruses. He even affirmed that I wanted my people to live godly lives. But he feared that the Chapel would change and that what it had stood for across the years would be lost.

Those were good men, all of them Christians, and included some of the best and most godly I have ever known. That is what made it all so difficult. Those who affirmed me as a man of God affirmed them as well. The tension was high and was without question the greatest crisis in Westminster Chapel's history.

But it was brilliant for me. It might be an exaggeration to say it was the *best* thing that ever happened to me, but it was certainly one of the best. All I had preached I now had to practise to the hilt. It refined me, embarrassed me, shaped me, exposed how weak I was. But God not only did not desert me but was more gracious and real than ever. I wouldn't want to go through it again but its value to me was, literally, more precious than gold.

I dare say those men could claim the same thing. They too would avow that God allowed it for a purpose and that they are all the better for it. They were *not* like Saul. God doesn't necessarily need a Saul to refine his servants. But God used Saul to mould David.

The challenge of having a secret anointing – known to you and a few others – is that you have to wait a long time for your time to come. Many fall by the wayside because they cannot wait.

I once watched a high-profile man reach the top only to tumble. He was a good man, but success went to his head. I wrote him a letter and quoted what Dr Lloyd-Jones once said to me: 'The worst thing that can happen to a man is to succeed before he is ready.' The man replied to my letter, claimed he agreed with it, and promised to lie low – postponing the high profile again until God was ready to use him as before. It is painful to have to wait, especially if one has been acclaimed – like David – then has to wait.

David had done nothing wrong. He hadn't flaunted a coat of many colours – like Joseph who only egged on his brothers to be jealous. David was solid gold but still needed refining. He was a humble man. He didn't feel worthy to marry the king's daughter. He was guileless. He didn't know that Saul's proposition – bring a hundred Philistine foreskins – was a trap to have David killed by the Philistines. But David brought in two hundred and accepted the gift of Saul's daughter for a wife. 'Saul became still more afraid of him, and he remained his enemy for the rest of his days' (1 Sam. 18:29).

The secret anointing in you, though you are kept from a high profile, will still be a threat to the enemy God chooses for your refinement. David could not hide his anointing. He wasn't ambitious. He simply did what he was asked to do and did it too well. In fact he had so much ability that God had to take him to the sidelines lest things be worse than ever.

Are you waiting for your time to come? You say, 'How long, O Lord?' (Ps. 13:1). David thought the preparation would never end. You may feel the same way. But thank God for the secret anointing in you. Thank God for friends. And thank God for your enemies. They will probably mean more to you, at the end of the day, than your friends!

Tomorrow's Man or Woman

Having the anointing but not the platform can be a very painful thing. I can recall those awful days – precious to me now but horrible then – when I had to sell vacuum cleaners to make a living. I was too deep in debt to be in full-time Christian work, so I had to knock on strangers' doors and talk my way into giving a demonstration of my vacuum cleaners (which they were not in the market for buying) so I could make a sale and pay my bills. I would go to church on Sundays and hear various speakers. 'Why can't I be up there preaching?' I would say to myself. Often I listened to people who seemed not to have great gifts, thinking 'I can preach better than that,' but *they* had the platform.

Waiting. And more waiting. Preparation – of the spirit, not just the intellect. Those were awful days but as essential to my getting ready as any class in seminary.

I write this for tomorrow's man or woman. You have that secret anointing. But no platform. Your time has not come. But time is on your side. What God has in mind for you is worth waiting for.

For David there was an unconscious preparation in his own household. 'A man's enemies will be the members of his own household' (Matt. 10:36). I wonder how it made him feel that his own father would never have sent for him had not Samuel kept pressing, 'Are these all the sons you have?' (1 Sam. 16:11). His father naturally hoped Samuel would anoint Eliab, the first-born. David was the 'runt of the litter', the youngest and most underestimated. Sometimes our parents, who tried the hardest on the oldest, take the younger ones for granted. In any case, it is painful when your own parent – mother or father – underestimates you. 'But the Lord looks at the heart' (1 Sam. 16:7). God saw in David what Jesse underestimated – a young man with a heart after God.

Do you know what it is like to live beneath your parents' expectation or approval? Do you feel pain as you wait for your time to come that is aggravated partly by a frustrated relationship with your father or mother? We all grow up wanting to please our parents. I'm not sure we ever outgrow that. As I write these lines my aged father, near ninety, has Alzheimer's. I can recall my last sane conversation with him, when he was verging on that disease, hoping to get a word of approval. As I said earlier, being in G Campbell Morgan's pulpit went a long way. But I still wanted more.

I have been brought up in a 'perfectionist' type of atmosphere. This is not only due to my Nazarene background (they emphasised John Wesley's teaching of Christian perfection) but because my own father clearly thought I would do just a little bit better than I did. My father was the greatest Christian I've ever known, and no human being on earth is more grateful than I for the kind of Dad I had, but he wasn't perfect. I can recall walking home from school at the age of eight, with a report card of all As but one B. I dreaded showing my Dad that report card because I knew he would focus on the one B. I was right. 'That's a good report card, son, but if you work a little harder you could have all As next time.' I did work harder and the next time I got all As but two A minuses. What do you suppose my dad focused on?

The feeling that we never come up to standard is frustrating.

I'm not saying that David felt like this. I only know his own father Jesse was ready to let Samuel go on his way without seeing David. David may well have got his sense of self-esteem from playing the harp and killing Goliath. Or, which is best of all, in God. 'As the deer pants for streams of water, so my soul pants for you, O God . . . Why are you downcast, O my soul? Why so disturbed within me? Put your hope in God, for I will yet praise him, my Saviour and my God' (Ps. 42:1,11).

I heard Gigi Tchividjian give a talk in which she admitted to little self-esteem. 'Whenever I was introduced I was referred to as Billy Graham's daughter, the wife of a Swiss psychiatrist or the mother of six children.' She concluded that she had no identity of her own but sought it and found it in Christ.

As God has earmarked you for a work in the future I would urge you to get your sense of self-esteem from knowing you please God alone. Just him. He isn't hard to please. First, the blood of Jesus washed all sin and imperfection away. Second, Jesus is at the Father's right hand and is moved with compassion over our weaknesses. Third, the Father in any case 'knows how we are formed, he remembers that we are dust' (Ps. 103:14).

It is true that God will refine you so that when your time has come you will be ready and trustworthy of a greater anointing. But you won't be perfect. Being perfect in love (1 John 4:18) won't mean you're absolutely perfect. 'If we claim to be without sin, we deceive ourselves and the truth is not in us' (1 John 1:8). In any case 'his commands are not burdensome' (1 John 5:3). God isn't waiting for you to get perfect before he can use you. Otherwise he wouldn't use anybody — ever.

Do you have a heart after God? Do you yearn to honour him? Do you aspire to seek not honour and glory from your peers but the honour that God alone can bestow? If so, God will find you. Your parents may not see in you what is there, however well they think they know you, but God does. He will find you. He will discover you. Someone said, 'It takes fifteen years to become an overnight success.' God's time has come when someone who knows all that is needed to know about you then steps in without your raising a finger. 'So he asked Jesse, "Are these all the sons you have?" "There is still the youngest," Jesse answered, "but he is tending the sheep." Samuel said, "Send for him; we will not sit down until he arrives" ' (1 Sam. 16:11).

But there was more unconscious preparation for David, tomorrow's servant of Christ. His own brothers were jealous of him. As I said earlier, unlike Joseph who tantalised his brothers with his ornamented coat and by revealing his dreams (Gen. 37:3–11), David was innocent. He did not deliberately make his brothers jealous. Jealousy among his brothers may have started when Samuel anointed him, but it came out when David, following his father's orders, went to the place of battle that led to the slaying of Goliath.

David was appalled when he saw how scared the Israelite army was over Goliath's threats. He only asked, 'Who is this uncircumcised Philistine that he should defy the armies of the living God?' It was a reasonable question to ask, especially by one who was convinced of the sovereignty and power of the living God. Mind you, David didn't say this to his brothers, as if to chide them or impress them. He said it to others. 'When Eliab, David's oldest brother, heard him speaking with the men, he burned with anger at him and asked, "Why have you come down here? And with whom did you leave those few sheep in the desert? I know how conceited you are and how wicked your heart is; you came down only to watch the battle" ' (1 Sam. 17:28). David knew he'd said the wrong thing in their eyes. ' "Now what have I done?" said David. "Can't I even speak?" ' (1 Sam. 17:29).

Sibling rivalry can be a refining process. And yet I have to say I know nothing of this. I was an only child until I was fifteen, so I know nothing of being the object of the jealousy of a brother or sister. In fact I was so oblivious to this sort of thing that I had difficulty in coming to terms with feeling this later on in life. But most grow up with it. And that David, the youngest child, should be chosen by Samuel, then be chiding Israelite officers for their lack of faith, got his brothers' goat. But that little bit of jealousy by comparison was also a bit of preparation for the day he would be the target of full-blown jealousy.

If you are tomorrow's man or woman, it is only a matter of time before people will be jealous of you. Perhaps you were underestimated by a perfectionist parent, perhaps a brother or sister has been jealous of you; such is the stuff of life that gets you ready for a battle ahead.

I remember hearing a preacher say long ago: 'Some are jealous of your face. Some are jealous of your lace. And some will be jealous of your grace.' The last form of jealousy is the worst; if that secret anointing is on you, you will see things, say things and be prepared to do things – all because of grace – which will stir up another's jealousy. People can't help it. And, by the way, *you're* no different!

How we respond to another's jealousy will determine whether we will truly come through as tomorrow's man or woman. It is what saved David and eventually made him great, although it could have been his undoing. I love the way the Authorised Version puts it: 'David behaved himself wisely in all his ways' (1 Sam. 18:14). When you know someone is jealous of you, you know you will have to be extremely shrewd. You never let them know you know what their problem is. You simply put it into your 'computer' and act accordingly – running for cover and, if possible, giving them no cause to speak against you. 'For it is God's will that by doing good you should silence the ignorant talk of foolish men' (1 Pet. 2:15). 'Who is going to harm you if you are eager to do good? But even if you should suffer for what is right, you are blessed. "Do not fear what they fear; do not be frightened" ' (1 Pet. 3:13–14).

There were basically two things on which David – tomorrow's man – would be tested. They would make his secret anointing stronger than ever, so that by the time that anointing became public and was given a platform it would be exactly what God envisaged.

The first test: sensitivity to grieving the Holy Spirit The Holy Spirit is a person. A very, very sensitive person at that. He gets his feelings hurt easily. You may say, 'That's not a very secure person.' Well, all I can say is that the Holy Spirit is very secure indeed but at the same time he can be grieved – hurt. 'And do not grieve the Holy Spirit of God, with whom you were sealed for the day of redemption' (Eph. 4:30).

Early on in my ministry at Westminster Chapel I came to explore this teaching. It probably began when I was a child. The first preacher that I can remember was Dr Gene Phillips, my pastor in Ashland, Kentucky. He may have had deeper influence on shaping me than any other minister. He would often warn about 'grieving the Holy Ghost'. That made an indelible impression on me and I never got over it. For grieving the Holy Spirit is not something anybody should want to do, and a person with an anointing without the platform must learn, sooner or later, (1) that the Holy Spirit can be grieved, (2) that he can be easily grieved and (3) that we must learn how *not* to grieve him. But I have grieved the Spirit countless times, I am ashamed to say; and yet I have learned in some ways over the years how not to grieve him. So early in my ministry in London I began seriously to explore this.

We almost never know at the time we grieve the Spirit. It is like when Samson gave his secret (why he had such enormous strength) to Delilah. She finally persuaded him to reveal why he was so strong. 'With such nagging she prodded him day after day until he was tired to death' (Judg. 16:16). Samson's weakness was women (Judg. 16:1). But when he fell in love with Delilah, not knowing it was a satanic trap, he feared losing her. Then came those sad words: 'So he told her everything. "No razor has ever been used on my head," he said, "because I have been a Nazirite set apart to God since birth. If my head were shaved, my strength would leave me, and I would become as weak as any other man"' (Judg. 16:17). The result: he lost his anointing temporarily and was as weak as a kitten. These words tell us a lot about the grieved Holy Spirit: 'But he did not know that the LORD had left him' (Judg. 16:20). In other words, when he revealed the secret of his anointing to Delilah he didn't feel a thing. But when he tried to do what he was always able to do before, he was utterly powerless. And yet the departure of the anointing was painless and without any conscious feeling.

I have learned the same thing. When I grieve the Spirit – whether by losing my temper or speaking about someone in an unflattering manner – I feel nothing. In fact it almost always seems right at the time! We feel justified. Right. It may take hours or days – sometimes years – before we admit we grieved the Spirit.

What happens is this. When I grieve the Holy Spirit, he slips away without my knowing it. Like a gentle dove – who *remained* on Jesus (John 1:32) but not on me – he unobtrusively flutters away. The Holy Spirit leaves no hint that he has done that. We find out later on.

If a goal of spirituality is partly to close the time gap between the moment when we *observe* the manifestation of the Spirit and our actual *affirmation* of it, so likewise must tomorrow's servant of Christ learn to close the time gap between sin and repentance. In other words, how long does it take to tell that grieving the Spirit is precisely what I did? It may take years before I come to terms with a wrong attitude. It may take months before I admit I got it wrong. It may take days. Or hours. Or seconds. If you and I can learn to close the time gap to a few seconds, we are getting close to enjoying continuity of the ungrieved Spirit indwelling us. The goal: no discontinuity in our relationship with the ungrieved Spirit; that we do *not* grieve him. By holding a grudge. A curt, flippant word. A tongue that hurts another's credibility. I could go on and on. It is *so* easy to do. But it grieves the Spirit.

The chief way we grieve the Spirit is by bitterness. A bitter spirit – that always seems right at the time. We feel nothing. The backslider in heart is always 'filled with his own ways' (Prov. 14:14 AV). It seems right when we are bitter. Totally justified in our own hearts. But the Spirit has excused himself, possibly only to return when we put things right.[1] The first thing Paul mentions, having admonished that we should not grieve the Spirit, is bitterness: 'Get rid of all bitterness, rage and anger, brawling and slander, along with every form of malice. Be kind and compassionate to one another, forgiving each other, just as in Christ God forgave you' (Eph. 4:31–2).

David had reached the place in his spiritual pilgrimage where he recognised in *minutes* if not *seconds* when he grieved the Holy Spirit. An unexpected opportunity was handed to David. When Saul learned that David was in En Gedi, Saul went there. David and his men were far back in a cave. David's followers saw this as a moment he could gain Saul's throne. 'The men said, "This is the day the LORD spoke of when he said to you, 'I will give your enemy into your hands for you to deal with as you wish.'" ' Then David crept up unnoticed and cut off a corner of Saul's robe' (1 Sam. 24:4).

There was a severe test. Instead of killing Saul David decided to be content with leaving his footprints. He crept up unnoticed and cut off a corner of Saul's robe. That seemed an innocuous thing to do. But 'afterwards David was conscience-stricken for having cut off a corner of his robe' (1 Sam. 24:5). This act may seem harmless to some but not to David. His walk with the Lord during those days of heart-preparation had led him to a highly developed sensitivity to what grieves the Spirit. I say, many would have thought nothing of this.

But David felt terrible. 'He said to his men, "The LORD forbid that I should do such a thing to my master, the LORD's anointed, or lift my hand against him; for he is the anointed of the LORD." With these words David rebuked his men and did not allow them to attack Saul. And Saul left the cave and went his way' (1 Sam. 24:6–7).

Tomorrow's servant of Christ learns to recognise the Holy Spirit and sense the things which grieve him. We must learn to close the time gap from years to seconds, as David seems to have done. David immediately wished he hadn't done that. Tomorrow's man or woman must develop such intimacy with the Holy Spirit that they can tell what grieves him and when it happens.

It is so easy to say an ungracious thing about someone, especially if we feel they are up to no good. We may feel innocent when we go to another, 'Let me tell you about so-and-so. I am telling you this for your own good.' I don't rule out that there are times when one must be warned (cf. 3 John 9ff.), but if we aren't careful we will justify this sort of thing every time we open our mouths – then wonder why we've got no power!

Some time ago Louise and I had an argument on a Saturday morning. It wasn't the first, nor the last! But on that day I thought she was horrible! She thought I was! I went upstairs to prepare a sermon. No thoughts came. Nothing. I was so angry. I said, 'Lord, you've got to help me, I've got to preach tomorrow.' Silence. No thoughts or insight. No frame of reference from the text I was going to preach from so I could make an outline. Utter silence from heaven. The hours rolled by. 'God, you put me in Westminster Chapel, now help me!' Silence. All day long my greatest fear was that I'd have to apologise. But I can't do that! She was in the wrong! I kept trying to prepare. It was now five o'clock, time was running out. I knew what I had to do. I knew all along. My pride kept me from giving in so I dug in my heels. Six o'clock. No thoughts. Nothing. I went downstairs to where Louise was in the kitchen. 'I'm sorry, it's all my fault.' We embraced and wept. I went back upstairs, sat in the same chair and turned to the same Bible. I promise you, in forty-five minutes I had everything I needed for Sunday morning's sermon! The thoughts poured so fast I could hardly write them all down! The explanation: the ungrieved Spirit began to flow in me. The Spirit was allowed to be himself in me.

The second test: refusing to vindicate oneself This was at stake when David was given the chance to kill the king. He refused. He passed the test. But he felt so horrible over cutting a piece off Saul's robe that he welcomed an opportunity to prove he wouldn't do that.

That opportunity came. Saul learned that David was now hiding on the hill of Hakilah and hurried there. David saw Saul first and came to him when the king was fast asleep. 'Abishai said to David, "Today God has delivered your enemy into your hands. Now let me pin him to the ground with one thrust of my spear; I won't strike him twice" ' (1 Sam. 26:8). David would not allow it, and refused to touch Saul in any way. God gave him a second chance. He passed the test. 'But David said to Abishai, "Don't destroy him! Who can lay a hand on the LORD's anointed and be guiltless?" ' (1 Sam. 26:9). *No cutting of Saul's robe this time*.

And yet the real issue here is the matter of vindication. David had an opportunity to have his own platform – it was at his fingertips. But he refused. He did not want to be responsible for vindicating himself.

Every servant of Christ must pass this test. 'Do not take revenge, my friends, but leave room for God's wrath, for it is written: "It is mine to avenge; I will repay," says the Lord' (Rom. 12:19). Vindication is God's act. It is what he does best! The one thing he *doesn't* want is our help. Indeed, if we pull strings to advance ourselves – as if to help God out – God will back off, leave it to us to that we may see what a mess we will make of things.

Tomorrow's man or woman must not pull strings to get to where he or she wants. David was governed by the principle of non-vindication when it came to his personal interests. His rationale was this:

'As surely as the LORD lives,' he said, 'the LORD himself will strike him; either his time will come and he will die, or he will go into battle and perish. But the LORD forbid that I should lay a hand on the Lord's anointed. Now get the spear and water jug that are near his head, and let's go.' (1 Sam. 26:10–11)

But David wasn't perfect. Had not Abigail intervened when her husband Nabal was on David's hit list, David would have had blood on his hands (1 Sam. 25:12–34). He was spared this guilt at the last minute.

David said to Abigail, 'Praise be to the LORD, the God of Israel, who has sent you today to meet me. May you be blessed for your good judgment and for keeping me from bloodshed this day and from avenging myself with my own hands. Otherwise, as surely as the LORD, the God of Israel, lives, who has kept me from harming you, if you had not come quickly to meet me, not one male belonging to Nabal would have been left alive by daybreak.' (1 Sam. 25:32–4)

Every servant of Christ, if honest, can testify to God's gracious intervention that keeps him or her from grievous sin. It is by the sheer grace of God that any of us is kept from scandalous sin. David knew that so well. Do we?

We don't usually know that we are being tested and that God and the angels are watching. A satanic trap can be God's set-up – whether it be holding a grudge, vindicating ourselves or sexual temptation – to see whether we really will become tomorrow's men and women.

David eventually was ready. His secret anointing turned into an outward anointing (2 Sam. 2:4) and David was given a platform to use his many gifts. He became the greatest king Israel ever had.

It was a long wait. Nearly twenty years transpired between David's secret anointing (1 Sam. 16:13) and his public anointing (2 Sam. 2:4). But it was worth waiting for. Tomorrow's man became today's man.

13

Openness to God's Word

> Thou hast magnified thy word above all thy name. (Ps. 138:2 AV)

It will be recalled from my Introduction that tomorrow's anointing will result in the combination of the word and the Spirit. The preparation that God provides for tomorrow's servant of Christ has as part of its aim making him or her open and obedient to the Spirit.

The anointing on David would take him beyond his musicianship and bravery. The Spirit of the Lord was on him to write many psalms. Jesus confirmed that David's psalms were 'by the Spirit' (Matt. 22:43). In these psalms David reveals his love for God's word and says that the Lord's commands and ordinances are:

> More precious than gold,
>   than much pure gold;
> they are sweeter than honey,
>   than honey from the comb.
> By them is your servant warned;
>   in keeping them there is great reward.
>   (Ps. 19:10–11)

It was the anointing on David by which he saw that God

himself magnified his word above his own name (Ps. 138:2).[1] The NIV says, 'You have exalted above all things your name and your word' – which of course is true. For the two ways God has revealed himself in scripture are through his word and through his name.

But why would David actually say that God magnified his word above all his name? I believe the explanation is this: God puts priority on his integrity over his reputation. The Bible is God putting his integrity on the line. He certainly cares about the honour of his name – of course he does – but it is the integrity of what he *says* about himself and what he *promises* to do that he puts first in order of priority.

God's *name* actually points to two things: his power and his honour. When Peter took advantage of a miraculous healing to preach the Gospel he said, 'Men of Israel, why does this surprise you? Why do you stare at us as if by our own power or godliness we had made this man walk?' (Acts 3:12). Peter then referred to the God of Abraham, Isaac and Jacob. God had revealed himself to the patriarchs as God Almighty, but 'by my *name* the LORD I did not make myself known to them' (Exod. 6:3).

I find this rather extraordinary: to think that the name of the Lord had not been truly unveiled to the patriarchs (Abraham, Isaac and Jacob) but first revealed to Moses. The way to be *saved* was first revealed to Abraham (Gen. 15:6), who became Paul's chief example of justification by faith alone. The Gospel was revealed to Abraham (Gal. 3:8), and all we need to know about salvation was shown to Abraham – four hundred years *before* the time of Moses.

How did God reveal himself to Abraham? By his *word*. Just the word. That is the way we are saved to this day – by hearing the word.

But what does it say? 'The word is near you; it is in your mouth and in your heart,' that is, the word of faith we are proclaiming: That if you confess with your mouth, 'Jesus is

Lord,' and believe in your heart that God raised him from the dead, you will be saved. (Rom. 10:8–9)

How, then, can they call on the one they have not believed in? And how can they believe in the one of whom they have not heard? And how can they hear without someone preaching to them. (Rom. 10:14)

Consequently, faith comes from hearing the message, and the message is heard through the word of Christ. (Rom. 10:17)

This tells us that the Gospel is complete *without* signs and wonders. We are saved by faith alone in God's word – alone.

This helps to explain why God magnifies his word above all his name. But with the disclosure of the name of the LORD came the unprecedented phenomena of signs, wonders and miracles. The power therefore unveiled under Moses' anointing was now transferred to the name of Jesus. So Peter could say, 'Silver or gold I do not have, but what I have I give you. In the name of Jesus Christ of Nazareth, walk' (Acts 3:6). Thus the power inherent in the name of the LORD was now invested in the name of Jesus. 'By faith in the name of Jesus, this man whom you see and know was made strong. It is Jesus' name and the faith that comes through him that has given this complete healing to him, as you can all see' (Acts 3:16).

The Gospel is complete without signs and wonders but the Bible is not complete without signs and wonders. And yet signs and wonders came later – at the same time as God revealed his *name*. We therefore have every right to connect God's name to signs and wonders.

So the name referred to God's honour and reputation. 'You shall not misuse the name of the LORD your God, for the LORD will not hold anyone guiltless who misuses his name' (Exod. 20:7). 'I am the LORD; that is my name! I will not give my glory to another or my praise to idols' (Isa. 42:8). When God was angry with the children of Israel in the desert he offered to destroy them and start all over with Moses. But Moses pleaded that God would not do this and reminded him that his honour and reputation were at stake:

> Moses said to the LORD, 'Then the Egyptians will hear about it! By your power you brought these people up from among them. And they will tell the inhabitants of this land about it. They have already heard that you, O LORD, are with these people and that you, O LORD, have been seen face to face, that your cloud stays over them, and that you go before them in a pillar of cloud by day and a pillar of fire by night. If you put these people to death all at one time, the nations who have heard this report about you will say, "The LORD was not able to bring these people into the land he promised them on oath; so he slaughtered them in the desert." ' (Num. 14:13–16)

God relented. He cares about the honour of his name. But he cares even more about his integrity – which is his word. This is why Psalm 138:2 says that God has magnified his word over all his name. Speaking on this verse, I love the way Adonica Howard-Browne put it: 'You can trust his word and you can trust his name. *Your name is only as good as your word. If you don't keep your word then you won't have a good name.* If you do business with somebody and they don't keep their word you'll tell people not to go there, but if they are good you will tell people that's where they ought to buy.'

Signs, wonders and miracles, then, were first unveiled in the Bible when God revealed his name to Moses (Exod. 6:2–3). Yet God wants his word to be magnified above signs and wonders. Salvation is more important than miracles. Salvation was thus unveiled to Abraham four hundred years before the era of signs and wonders. We are not saved by signs and wonders but by the Gospel.

We have to be careful therefore to walk in obedience to every word. Jesus said that 'everything' must be fulfilled that is written about him in the Law, the prophets and the psalms (Luke 24:44). 'Not the least stroke of a pen' would be omitted from the fulfilment of the Law (Matt. 5:18). This shows how clearly and carefully God regards *every word* he utters. Paul wanted what he wrote to be acknowledged as the Lord's command (1 Cor. 14:37).

I suspect that some of us think that the only way God can 'restore the honour of his name', to quote Graham Kendrick's great hymn, is by signs and wonders. That *may* work. Indeed, when the forty-year-old man who had never walked was healed the people were 'filled with wonder and *amazement*' (Acts 3:10). When Jesus healed a boy with an evil spirit 'they were all *amazed* at the greatness of God' (Luke 9:43). And yet the exact same word, *ekplesso*, is used to describe the effect of Jesus' words when he finished the Sermon on the Mount. 'When Jesus had finished saying these things, the crowds were *amazed* at his teaching, because he taught as one who had authority, and not as their teachers of the law' (Matt. 7:28–9). This shows that Jesus could *amaze* people by his *word* as easily as by signs and wonders! Indeed, when he put the Sadducees in their place the crowds 'were *astonished* [same Greek word] by his *teaching*' (Matt. 22:33).

If Jesus could amaze and astonish either by his word or by miracles it seems to me that this should happen today as well. But we apparently have lost faith in the power of the word and fancy that miraculous healings alone can restore God's honour. In my opinion, either should do this.

Every generation has its stigma by which the believer's faith is tested. Yesterday's stigma is easily accepted today. We may think we are being sufficiently open to the word merely because we accept yesterday's stigma. If we extol great servants like Augustine or Luther, Wesley or Smith-Wigglesworth, we may suppose we are bearing today's stigma. But the Pharisees felt the same way. The Pharisees felt righteous because they affirmed yesterday's prophets. 'Woe to you, teachers of the law and Pharisees, you hypocrites! You build tombs for the prophets and decorate the graves of the righteous. And you say, "If we had lived in the days of our forefathers, we would not have taken part with them in shedding the blood of the prophets" ' (Matt. 23:29–30). But Jesus exposed their hypocrisy by adding: 'So you testify against yourselves that you are the descendants of those who murdered the prophets. Fill up, then, the measure of the sin of your forefathers!' (Matt. 23:31–2).

In other words, the Pharisees displayed their superficiality by rejecting the stigma of their own day, namely Jesus the promised Messiah right before their eyes! The task of every generation is to discern in which direction the Sovereign Redeemer is moving, then to move in that direction. This comes by being open to the word and the Holy Spirit. The Holy Spirit's direction is always a fresh stigma, injuring our pride and challenging our sophistication. 'But God chose the foolish things of the world to shame the wise; God chose the weak things of the world to shame the strong. He chose the lowly things of this world and the despised things – and the things that are not – to nullify the things that are' (1 Cor. 1:27–8). We must never forget that today's challenge will make us look stupid to most people.

There are those of us who feel we are already sufficiently open to the word. Many of us feel we are most certainly open to the Holy Spirit. Some of us feel that if we have the word we therefore have the Spirit – and need not be bothered about being further open to the Spirit. On the other hand, some of us feel that since we have the Spirit it proves that we have the word; we therefore need not worry over whether we are further open to the word.

Another issue is the Bible's infallibility. If we doubt the inerrancy of the word, we are less likely to be open to it. Why be open to the Bible if it is not absolutely God's word? We must be convinced that the Bible is God's own word. I would point the reader to Wayne Grudem's *Systematic Theology* because Dr Grudem is a theologian truly open to the Spirit and makes the case for biblical infallibility I don't have space for here.[2]

Why is this chapter so important? I believe there has been a silent divorce in the church between the word and the Spirit. Because there are those on the 'word' side saying: the need of the hour is for preaching of the Bible generally and expository preaching particularly; we must earnestly contend for the faith once for all entrusted to the saints (Jude 3); we need to recover the Reformation heritage – centred on the Gospel. There are those on the 'Spirit' side saying: the need today is for signs and wonders; the world will not be shaken until we recover apostolic power; we need to see healings and prophetic words which will show the world that the Church is alive.

What is wrong with either emphasis? Nothing. Both are right. There is a need for a remarriage of the word and Spirit.

What I want to do now is to suggest how we might see how open we really are. It is one thing for me to say, 'I know I am open to the word.' But am I? Am I open in my *heart* or just in my *head*?

I have travelled quite a bit, preaching on both sides of the Atlantic, in Europe, the Far East, Africa, Australia and other places. I have done a lot of listening as well as preaching. Let me list what I have observed.

Some seem more interested in God's secret will than they are in his revealed will Let me explain. God's revealed will is the Bible. The Old Testament includes the Law, prophets, psalms (Luke 24:44). The New Testament includes the teachings of Jesus, acts of the Church, and the epistles: doctrine. God's secret will refers to direct guidance.[3] 'What does God want me to do today?' 'Whom should I marry?' 'Where should I go to church?' 'Will I get this job?' 'Should I move house?'

God has a secret will for each of us. We are all interested in this and there is nothing wrong with wanting to know specifically what God wants us to do. But this interest often amounts to wanting a short cut, like eating in a fast-food place when you're in a hurry. A long-term interest in teaching and preaching shows you want to know God for his own sake.

Some seem more interested in the prophetic word than the preached word Preaching is God's way of saving people and teaching them (1 Cor. 1:21). This means preaching from the Bible, explaining the Bible, exploring the Bible. The prophetic word refers to 'Thus saith the Lord'. Giving a word of knowledge, telling a person what God wants to do for him or her, giving specific advice in a critical situation.

A prophetic word is exciting. Who among us isn't interested in this if we feel it is really from God? But this is no sign of a true spiritual appetite. It could stem from either selfishness or curiosity. When I announce that Paul Cain is going to preach the crowds swell noticeably. Not because they are really interested in his preaching but they love to hear him prophesy to people. I do understand this but it is not necessarily healthy.

Some seem more interested in manifestations of the Spirit than they are in the Gospel Manifestations (how the Spirit shows himself) may include falling down, laughter, signs and wonders, unusual prophetic words of knowledge. The Gospel explains who Jesus is and why he came, what he did on the cross and why, how people are saved.

This is a rather serious observation indeed. I don't mean to be unfair, but the danger here is that people are obsessed with manifestations and too often carry a minimal burden for the lost. I even fear that the Gospel is sometimes 'tacked on' and brought in grudgingly. Sometimes the Gospel isn't even preached at all. If so, could this be right?

Some seem more interested in the gifts of the Spirit than in the fruits of the Spirit Gifts usually refer to speaking in tongues, prophecy, word of knowledge, etc. (1 Cor. 12:8–10). Fruits refer to love, joy, peace, etc. (Gal. 5:22ff.).

Some seem more interested in being inwardly blessed and continually receiving personal help than in saving the lost They love worship and praise, feeling the presence of God. Saving the lost means reaching the unchurched and leading a soul to Christ, seeing conversions.

Some Christians seem to be preoccupied with experience and feeling rather than with teaching and doctrine God made us with emotions and feelings. A true encounter with God affects the whole person. One therefore experiences and feels God. The witness of the Spirit is *felt*.

I also sympathise with the view that some of us – I know I do – need a 'head bypass operation'. We can be so cerebral and intellectual that theological orthodoxy becomes everything. But God also gave us minds. To defend the faith requires thinking. We therefore must prove our openness to the word by knowing what we believe.

Some seem more interested in public worship than in private quiet times By public worship I mean singing, open praying, prayer groups. By private quiet time I refer to reading the Bible daily, time alone with God, developing intimacy with God.

I *do* wish I were wrong about this. But I know too much. Some Christian leaders not only say little about a Christian's quiet time with the Lord but, in some cases, even imply that it isn't too important. I think this is wrong. Reader, may I ask: how much do you pray? How much actual time do you spend alone with God each day? I don't refer to 'praying without ceasing', which some claim to do day and night as if this compensates for setting a regular time each day to be alone with God.

There will be no praying in heaven. When you stand before the Lord you may well regret how you used so much of your time, but I can safely promise that you will not regret a single minute you spent alone with God. For what it's worth, I recommend no less than thirty minutes a day in prayer and Bible reading. Church leaders, I personally believe, should spend at least twice that amount of time alone with the Lord.

Apart from how you are going to feel before the Lord Jesus at his Judgment Seat, have you any idea what private prayer may have to do with your increased anointing? It could mean *everything*. I would be *afraid* to ask God for more anointing and then not seek his face daily with all my heart.

The first time Paul Cain spoke at Westminster Chapel he gave this advice to us: seek God's face, not his hand. Seeking God's face means you want to know him, in intimacy; seeking his hand is only asking him to do things for you.

The above seven suggestions may indicate whether you and I are truly open to the word. I am convicted by these suggestions. I have taken counsel from a wide range of church leaders. It seems to me that these seven observations are tests to expose whether or not we are truly open to the word.

To put it the other way around, are there positive evidences that we are open to the word? I believe so. Consider these propositions:

We must affirm the full inspiration of the Bible The Holy Spirit wrote the Old Testament. 'All Scripture is God-breathed and is useful for teaching, rebuking, correcting and training in righteousness' (2 Tim. 3:16). 'God-breathed' is a direct reference to the Holy Spirit. 'And with that he breathed on them and said, "Receive the Holy Spirit" ' (John 20:22). 'For prophecy never had its origin in the will of man, but men spoke from God as they were carried along by the Holy Spirit' (2 Pet. 1:21). The whole of the Bible can be called 'prophecy'. All the writers wrote what they did because God prophetically spoke as they wrote under the Spirit's direct guidance. Affirming the scriptures is therefore affirming the prophetic words or word of knowledge that were given to the Old Testament writers. Whether it was Moses, David or Isaiah, all had words of knowledge given them by the Spirit to put pen to papyrus. It is one thing, then, to accept a word of knowledge for someone today – to which we must always be open (1 Thess. 5:20); it is *always* safe to accept the scriptures.

The Holy Spirit wrote the New Testament. The Holy Spirit makes that claim for the New Testament. 'He writes the same way in all his letters, speaking in them of these matters. His letters contain some things that are hard to understand, which ignorant and unstable people distort, *as they do the other Scriptures*, to their own destruction' (2 Pet. 3:16). 'For the Scripture says, "Do not muzzle the ox while it is treading out the grain," and "The worker deserves his wages" ' (1 Tim. 5:18). Here Paul quotes Jesus' words as found in Luke 10:7 and calls them 'scripture'. Paul claims this authority for himself as well. 'If anybody thinks he is a prophet or spiritually gifted, let him acknowledge that what I am writing to you is the Lord's command' (1 Cor. 14:37). In 1 Corinthians 7:6, Paul speaks as a concession, not as a command. This further shows that, whereas he is stating his godly opinion at places in 1 Corinthians 7, all other places *are* by 'command' and therefore under the Spirit's inspiration.

We must esteem the word as the Lord himself does The psalmist therefore acknowledges that God has magnified his word *above* all his name (Ps. 138:2 AV)! This means we should give priority to the written word over a prophetic word or word of knowledge. We must also reject any word of knowledge which is contrary to the written word. We must not go by our 'feelings' or how we 'feel led' if those feelings go against the written word. This could be painful. But it will show to what degree we esteem God's own written word.

We must be open to truth we may not want to be true As long as we use the Bible to prove what we have already decided is true, we will make little advance in our growth. It may be easier to accept as 'truth' what we are at home with, but the flesh (our human nature) could be the real motivation here. When we refer to certain verses in the Bible merely to uphold our 'party line' we are using the Bible no differently from the Pharisees or Sadducees.

We all need help here. I am vulnerable here. Once we have taken a stand on some theological premiss, especially when we have gone to print on it, it becomes much more difficult to change our point of view. I have had to admit to my *hoping* this or that teaching is not true. But I equally know that God will not give me an ever-increasing anointing if my mind is shut down to truth I hope isn't true.

Openness to the word therefore means I will follow truth wherever it leads me, however embarrassing it may be or with whomsoever I may have to disagree. 'How can you believe if you accept praise from one another, yet make no effort to obtain the praise that comes from the only God?' (John 5:44). That verse, more than any other in the Bible, has been my governing text in life. It isn't easy. But if I am hearing from the God of the Bible – the Creator and Father of the Lord Jesus Christ – all the pain and embarrassment is worth it. For the reward is always a greater anointing – precisely what this book is about. I don't want to become yesterday's man.

Will we regard a conversion to Christ as the greatest miracle? Conversion is a work of the Holy Spirit. As much power is needed to convert as to raise the dead or heal the blind or deaf. After all, that is what conversion does. It raises the dead (Eph. 2:1–8), heals the blind (2 Cor. 4:4–5), heals the deaf (Matt. 13:13–15). Conversion takes place because of the preaching of the Gospel (1 Cor. 1:21). The Gospel is the good news that Jesus Christ, the God-man, has paid our debt on the cross.

We must give the Gospel priority over manifestations of the Spirit This does not mean that we reject manifestations of the Spirit or that we are uninterested in them. But if they become our preoccupation we have unspiritual priorities.

We must regard soul-winning as more important than changing another Christian to our point of view Those who are strong on their emphasis on the word are often guilty at this point. I fear there are Christians who get far more excited over changing a person theologically than seeing a person come to Christ. Indeed, some are brilliant at theology who have yet to lead a soul to Christ. Likewise there are those, red-hot on the things of the Spirit, who get more excited over leading a person to speak in tongues than they are over witnessing to the lost.

Some people, I fear, right in the Church, do not grasp this or see the implications of the miraculous nature of conversion. This presupposes an evangelistic concern. We should love evangelism as much as we do seeing other Christians blessed. We should be as zealous to see the lost saved as some are eager to see their fellow Christians open to the Spirit. We should likewise desire the fruit of the Spirit as much as we do the gifts of the Spirit.

Are we prepared to admit we have not been as open to the word as we should have been? We surely want everybody to be open to the Spirit as well as to the word. Our prayer: that we are so equally open to the word and Spirit that it is impossible to say which excites us more.

14

Openness to the Holy Spirit

Do not cast me from your presence
  or take your Holy Spirit from me.
Restore to me the joy of your salvation
  and grant me a willing spirit, to sustain me.
                                    (Ps. 51:11–12)

The secret of David's success and usefulness is the Holy Spirit. He experienced the Holy Spirit in power from the moment Samuel discovered him as tomorrow's man (1 Sam. 16:13). Psalm 51 is a reminder that tomorrow's man or woman will not be perfect, although it must be our prayer day and night that you and I will be kept from the sin that lay behind that psalm.[1] But what strikes me is David's consciousness of having grieved the Spirit by his sin; hence the prayer of Psalm 51.

I am also gripped by his plea, 'Grant me a willing spirit', a clear indication of his openness to the Spirit. David did not want to miss anything that could be of God. A willing spirit, what he went on to call 'a broken spirit' (Ps. 51:17), is required of tomorrow's servant of the Lord if our anointing will be useful to God.

Before I proceed in this chapter I need to spell out one of the differences between being open to the word and being open to the Spirit. Openness to the word is but to be open to the Spirit *indirectly*. This is because the word – to which we must remain open – is powerful to us only when it is applied by the Spirit.

Let me put it another way. I have concluded that some very orthodox people (meaning 'sound' theologically) only have a soteriological view of the Holy Spirit. Soteriology (from the Greek *soter*, 'salvation') refers to the doctrine of salvation. This means that what Jesus did for us on the cross must be applied by the Holy Spirit. If the Gospel is not *applied* by the Spirit nobody will be saved. This is partly what I mean by a sound theology. It also means one has a sound doctrine of the Spirit.

But that is not the whole story, for there is more. Being open to the Spirit is being vulnerable to him immediately and directly. Being open to the word directly is to be open to the Spirit indirectly – as the Spirit applies that word. But being open to the Spirit is when he manifests himself in an *immediate and direct* manner.[2] That is what the present chapter is about.

Some of us find it easier to be open to the word than to the Holy Spirit. We feel *safe* with the word but fearful that the Holy Spirit may lead us out of our comfort zone. But the Holy Spirit to whom we should be open is the Author of the Bible and he will not lead us in any way that is contrary to what he has written through his sovereign instruments. We are as safe with the Spirit as we are with the word. And yet if we are not open to the Spirit we will likely never experience some of the very same things described in the word.

A lot has to do with our background, culture and temperament when it comes to this matter of openness. The older Christian who is a bit intellectual, middle-class or from a church which is more theological in emphasis, may gravitate towards the type of church service that will centre on a solid Bible study. The Christian, whether young or old, who may not be very intellectual by nature, or middle-class, is sometimes seen as more open to the Spirit – and it may have nothing to do with one's spirituality. There are people who would rather watch television than read a book before they became Christians. Conversion does not make a person like that intellectual any more than it will give a person a middle-class perspective. There are exceptions, of course; God can overrule anyone's temperament and background and revolutionise his or her intellectual interests. But it is unwise to ignore one's upbringing before conversion.

Those who are more open to the word than the Spirit, then, are not necessarily more godly. Those who are more open to the Spirit are not necessarily more godly.

I should hope, nonetheless, that those who by nature are more open to the Spirit would accept and the need for discipline and need for the word – and would take on board the suggestions I made in the previous chapter. Likewise I would hope that those more open to accept the word would see that they are no better off held captive to an intellectual approach to the Bible – and closing their minds and hearts to the Spirit.

Why are some people afraid of the Holy Spirit? Because the stigma of the Holy Spirit is his very presence. In other words, the stigma of the Spirit is the Spirit himself. He by nature *offends*; all that is offensive about the Father and the Son is embodied in the person of the Holy Spirit.

There is a stigma in each person of the Trinity. The offence of the Father is his prerogative – his right to do and say what he pleases. He is sovereign. He does what he does after the counsel of his own will. 'In him we were also chosen, having been predestined according to the plan of him who works out everything in conformity with the purpose of his will' (Eph. 1:11). 'For he says to Moses, "I will have mercy on whom I have mercy, and I will have compassion on whom I have compassion"' (Rom. 9:15; cf. Exod. 33:19). Said the psalmist, 'Our God is in heaven; he does whatever pleases him' (Ps. 115:3). This aspect of God offends.

But I do fear that the relative absence of any consciousness of the sovereignty of God in theology and practice today has taken its toll. The late John Wimber said he blamed himself for David Watson's death – that he didn't have enough faith. He may well have had insufficient faith, but faith is God's gift. God can give or withhold faith and be just either way. We cannot make God do anything. He has a will of his own. The only prayer God answers is what conforms to his will (1 John 5:14) and twisting his arm doesn't change what he wills. I greatly admired John Wimber and am deeply indebted to him. But I fear he imposed needless guilt on himself by assuming that we can claim God will heal everybody *we* want to be healed.

Many a sincere Christian has suffered pseudo-guilt for not having enough faith. If there is anything worse than that it is making a sick person feel guilty for remaining unwell because he or she does not have enough faith. God is sovereign. He is able to heal – make no mistake about that – but he reserves the right to determine when he manifests his glory by healing. We all have to die sooner or later. Great men and women of God like David Watson and John Wimber are taken home because God has greater need of them in heaven. We must allow God to have his pleasure in matters even though we ourselves are disappointed.

Each person of the Godhead has his own stigma and the stigma of the Father is his sovereign will. We must accept this truth about him and bow to him. 'Unless the LORD builds the house, its builders labour in vain. Unless the LORD watches over the city, the watchmen stand guard in vain' (Ps. 127:1).

The stigma of the Son is his provision – his death on the cross being the only way we can be saved. It is by Jesus' blood, more precious than anything in the history of the world. The same person who was accredited by God by signs, wonders and miracles was equally handed over to wicked men 'by God's set purpose and foreknowledge' (Acts 2:23). God raised Jesus from the dead and made him 'both Lord and Christ' (Acts 2:36). The result: 'Salvation is found in no one else, for there is no other name under heaven given to men by which we must be saved' (Acts 4:12). We are saved by what Christ did as long as it is joined by 'faith in his blood' (Rom. 3:25). This is why Jesus himself announced before his death, 'I am the way and the truth and the life. No-one comes to the Father except through me' (John 14:6).

The offence of the cross consists both in the way we are saved and that it is *only* through God's Son. That is the offence. This means all men and women are lost until they hear and receive the Gospel. This means they must hear the Gospel before they can receive it. 'How, then, can they call on the one they have not believed in? And how can they believe in the one of whom they have not heard? And how can they hear without someone preaching to them?' (Rom. 10:14). Even though signs, wonders and miracles continued after Jesus went to Heaven, the apostles never focused long on them but used the platform they provided to preach the Gospel. The forty-year-old lame man who was healed gave Peter a platform, not to push hard for more miracles but to proclaim the Gospel.

When Peter saw this, he said to them: 'Men of Israel, why does this surprise you? Why do you stare at us as if by our own power or godliness we had made this man walk? The God of Abraham, Isaac and Jacob, the God of our fathers, has glorified his servant Jesus. You handed him over to be killed, and you disowned him before Pilate, though he had decided to let him go. You disowned the Holy and Righteous One and asked that a murderer be released to you. You killed the author of life, but God raised him from the dead. We are witnesses of this. By faith in the name of Jesus, this man whom you see and know was made strong.

It is Jesus' name and the faith that comes through him that has given this complete healing to him, as you can all see.' (Acts 3:12–16)

The Gospel must sooner or later be central in any movement of the Holy Spirit that awakens the world. Manifestations of the Holy Spirit are one thing, seeing people come to Christ through the preaching of the cross is another. The former may give us a platform for preaching but if that platform is not stood on and taken advantage of for the sake of the Gospel and the lost there will be no real awakening.

We pray for signs and wonders in our church. We long for them. There are sick and disabled people – people in continual pain and discomfort – I want to see healed. But we have made a vow to God that, were he to bless us with signs, wonders and miracles in Westminster Chapel we would use the platform for the preaching of the Gospel. We actually did this publicly and formally recently. Following a Sunday evening service we held hands in a wide circle in the Chapel – from wall to wall and from the back of the church to the pulpit – pledging that if God would do this for us we would *always* keep the preaching of the Gospel central.

Each person of the Trinity, then, has his own stigma. And the stigma of the Spirit is his presence. The Holy Spirit offends. When one is offended by the Spirit it is because he is offended by God. It is not possible to find God pleasant but to find the Holy Spirit offensive. It is incongruous to affirm all that Jesus Christ was and did, then turn around and reject the Holy Spirit. The persons of the Godhead are united. Equally, each has his own stigma. The Holy Spirit mirrors the other persons of the Godhead; therefore how we respond to the person of the Spirit may show what we really feel about either the Father or the Son.

But since the Spirit can be offensive, why should we be open to him? Are we not foolish or irrational if we deliberately open ourselves to one who is offensive and who offends? Answer: we must affirm God as he is; the Holy Spirit is God. When our hearts are truly right with God we will find that God is not offensive at all! We will instead find him glorious! But we must take God as he is and be prepared to affirm the presence of the Holy Spirit – however God may sovereignly choose to reveal himself.

Not long ago I pleaded with a fellow minister, 'Stay open to the Holy Spirit.' He replied, 'I don't know what you mean by that.' Whether he was sincere or cynical in his reply, I want to show in this chapter what openness to the Holy Spirit is. But are there evidences that suggest one is more open to the word than the Spirit? I believe there are.

• Some Christians believe that the only prophetic word to-day comes through preaching. Some even say that the gift of prophecy in 1 Corinthians 12:10 is preaching – nothing more. They are comfortable, therefore, when the preached word is applied by the Spirit and they are *gripped*. But they are uneasy with a person giving a prophetic word of knowledge.

• Some Christians are enamoured with the Gospel but fearful concerning manifestations of the Spirit – whether tongues, prophecy, falling down or laughing. They love the Gospel with all their hearts and would die for it. But they are unhappy should there be anything that might suggest that manifestations of the Spirit are also from the Lord Jesus Christ.

• Some Christians are keen to manifest the fruits of the Spirit but have minimal interest in the gifts of the Spirit. They believe that to show love, joy and peace is more honouring to God than speaking in tongues. They have 1 Corinthians 13 to prove it! After all, Paul called love the most excellent way and clearly put the gifts in proper perspective.

- Some love doctrine and teaching and whatever stimulates the intellect but are suspicious of experience. They point out that Paul appealed to the mind and that any theology worth its salt requires that we grasp the content of the Gospel. Going by feelings and emotions is giving in to the flesh and doesn't require discipline.

- Some are not excited by public worship unless it focuses on the old hymns – at least a hundred years old. A modern hymn sometimes caters more to feeling than a sense of God's majesty. They believe real worship is done best during one's quiet time, and they come to church to praise God through hymns but mainly for preaching and teaching. They are quite put off by praying in small groups.

- Some are convinced that having the word is to have the Spirit in equal measure as well, therefore, any emphasis on the Spirit implies they don't already have the Spirit. They are so sure that we have all we need of the Spirit already, since every Christian has the Holy Spirit. Further openness to the Spirit is not only redundant but does not dignify the Spirit we have.

- Some Christians believe that any openness to the Spirit is opening oneself to what is not the Holy Spirit at all. Since all Christians have the Spirit it is dangerous to look beyond what God has already done in Christ. Otherwise we invite the flesh to take over, the worst-case scenario being that the devil and the occultic move in.

There, then, are some of the indications one is not very open to the Holy Spirit. A theological rationale lies behind most of this. But we must not forget temperament and background. And if one is by nature quite cerebral and intellectual, there is a genuine fear of letting any part of us that is not strictly the *mind* be involved.

But I should like to make the case that one be open to the Spirit – that is, more of the Holy Spirit. I too am an intellectual. Although my old background, to which I have referred in this book, has paved the way to this openness, I have been very, very cautious. But God has hemmed me in and I would address the reader who, if honest, has been fearful of the very openness I now espouse. True, every Christian has the Holy Spirit (Rom. 8:9). Moreover, we do not 'lack any spiritual gift' (1 Cor. 1:7). Indeed, we have been blessed 'with every spiritual blessing in Christ' (Eph. 1:3). But to the Corinthians Paul said 'Eagerly desire the greater gifts' (1 Cor. 12:31), which shows that his earlier word in 1 Corinthians 1:7 did not mean we have everything available already in an absolute sense. And to the Ephesians Paul hoped that they be 'filled with the Spirit' (Eph. 5:18), which must surely mean they might not always be – even though we are already blessed with every spiritual blessing!

What is openness to the Spirit?

- It is humility; the recognition that I don't have everything, I don't know everything. It is the awareness that I need more of the Holy Spirit.

- It is the self-conscious desire to find God wherever he is, to recognise him as soon as he appears and to miss nothing that could be received from him.

- It is knowing that God is willing to give me so much more as long as I admit my poverty as opposed to saying 'I do not need a thing' (Rev. 3:17). It is one thing for the Holy Spirit to open our hearts or our understanding; it is another for us to be open to him instead of challenging him to open us first. Admittedly, we have to be changed by God himself (by his sovereign power) before we are going to listen and obey. But is there not a case for our remaining open to the same Holy Spirit, having been converted, so that we miss nothing he would say to us? Answer: yes.

The underlying problem of the Hebrew Christians, to whom Hebrews is addressed, was that they had become 'hard of hearing' (Heb. 5:11 AV). This means they had become closed to the point of not even being able to hear God any more. They felt no need to be open.

The only link between us and the throne of grace is the Holy Spirit. If he is quenched or grieved we have cut off the only link that will let us know how God is moving today. We must therefore maintain the best possible relationship to the Spirit. Although God is the same yesterday, today and for ever, and therefore unchanging in his nature, he does not always reveal himself in one generation as he did in another. We must therefore be open to the Spirit lest we miss the way in which this God sovereignly chooses to manifest his glory.

• If we are closed (our minds fully made up) to whatever God may wish to do or say today we will miss his glory, just as Israel missed recognising the Messiah when he appeared. You could never have convinced the scribes, the priests or Pharisees that God's chosen Messiah would appear before their eyes – and they not see him! But this is what happened! If we are truly open to the Holy Spirit (because we are prepared to pay the price and go with whatever the stigma may be) there is probably more likelihood that we will not miss his glory when it is unveiled.

Every generation has its stigma by which the believer's faith is tested. It is not so difficult to believe what God did yesterday. But what God did yesterday was highly offensive at the time. We may say, 'I wouldn't have objected had I been alive then.' But the only proof that we would have accepted what God did in a previous generation is our affirming what God is doing in ours. Even the Pharisees felt themselves very pious because they affirmed yesterday's men! Jesus confronted them on this very issue. 'And you say, "If we had lived in the days of our forefathers, we would not have taken part with them in shedding the blood of the prophets" ' (Matt. 23:30). But they were committing the equivalent offence – rejecting Jesus Christ himself – in their own day. Jesus said to them, 'So you testify against yourselves that you are the descendants of those who murdered the prophets. Fill up, then, the measure of the sin of your forefathers!' (Matt. 23:31–2).

It is sometimes said that the good is the enemy of the best; a church that is reasonably prosperous doesn't want revival. I would not be surprised if Whitefield's followers today would have rejected George Whitefield himself! Or if Spurgeon's followers today would have rejected Charles Spurgeon himself!

• The offence in what God is doing in the present is almost always changed sufficiently from what he did previously in order to test one's love of God and true openness to the Spirit. As I said, not a single person listed in Hebrews 11 had the luxury of stepping into the stigma created by yesterday's man or woman of faith. All those described in Hebrews 11 were faced with a new and unprecedented stigma in their own generation. If you ask: 'How can I know I would qualify for a place in Hebrews 11 had I been living in ancient times?' I answer: if you embrace today's stigma you would have embraced whatever stigma there was in a previous day. You may say, 'I could never die like the martyrs of old.' I say: you would if you show today that you bear the stigma God puts before you. 'Whoever can be trusted with very little can also be trusted with much, and whoever is dishonest with very little will also be dishonest with much' (Luke 16:10).

Why be open to the Holy Spirit? Because God still speaks today. 'Today, if you hear his voice' (Ps. 95:7). But did this refer to the Holy Spirit? Yes.

> So, as the Holy Spirit says: 'Today, if you hear his voice, do not harden your hearts as you did in the rebellion, during the time of testing in the desert, where your fathers tested and tried me and for forty years saw what I did. That is why I was angry with that generation, and I said, "Their hearts are always going astray, and they have not known my ways." So I declared on oath in my anger, "They shall never enter my rest" ' (Heb. 3:7–11)

Some will say: surely the Bible is the infallible, inerrant and unchanging word of God, and this was given yesterday. I answer: God's word – the Bible – is infallible, inerrant and unchanging. And God gave us the Bible yesterday. But the Holy Spirit applies it today. And if we are open to the immediate and direct witness of the Spirit the Bible will be doubly real to us.

• The application of God's word by the Holy Spirit will be to focus on an aspect of that word which will be the offence of today. The Holy Spirit continues to speak – clearly, directly and immediately through prophecy, word of knowledge, vision and audible voice. But he will never, never, never conflict with or contradict anything in the Bible but only make it clearer!

  The Holy Spirit speaking today is *not* new revelation or in competition with the Bible. The proof of the Holy

Spirit's voice or manifestation will be that it vindicates and magnifies the Bible.

• Openness to the Holy Spirit is what will stand us in good stead not to miss what God is in today. There is no great stigma (speaking generally) in defending what Athanasius stood for. He stood alone – and won. But nobody will be ridiculed (that is, in the Church) for saying that Jesus Christ is truly God – co-eternal and co-substantial and co-equal with the Father. There is no great stigma in defending justification by faith alone today – even with many Roman Catholics. Martin Luther stood alone. But he won the day; today Christians generally grant that we are saved by faith alone in Christ's work on the cross. The stigma *may* repeat itself, however, and we must always be prepared to uphold the historic faith.

So one must not rule out that a challenge to an ancient truth once vindicated could re-emerge as a new battle that must be won. Remember, however, that the rule of thumb will be that the new stigma will be a *stigma* and it won't be easy to accept and stand for. The Holy Spirit will not deceive us. If we are on good terms with him, we will know what he is in and behind and what he is doing and saying. He is not likely to let those in whom he dwells ungrieved in large measure miss what is on the cutting edge, in Heaven's eyes.

What is openness to the Spirit? How may we *know* we are open, open in our hearts as well as our heads? It was Lydia's *heart* that the Lord opened (Acts 16:14). It is possible to be theoretically open (open in theory – that is, we give intellectual assent) but closed in our hearts. Why would we be open in the head but not the heart?

The chief impediment to openness to the Spirit is fear. 'For God did not give us a spirit of timidity, but a spirit of power, of love and of self-discipline' (2 Tim. 1:7). We must become vulnerable: able to be hurt, unprotected against attacks. Becoming vulnerable means that we are willing to be hurt – or embarrassed. We must cease protecting ourselves with things such as defence mechanisms (setting up defences in our minds) or excuses for not being involved or worrying about our reputation with friends – even closest friends.

We must learn to be extremely sensitive to the Spirit. The Holy Spirit is a person who can be grieved (Eph. 4:30) or quenched (1 Thess. 5:19). We grieve him chiefly by bitterness – having an unforgiving spirit (which is why we slander people; Eph. 4:30ff.). We quench the Spirit chiefly by protecting ourselves from vulnerability or speaking against what God is presently doing, supposing God couldn't be doing *that*! When the Spirit is unquenched *and* in us in large measure, which means we cultivate our relationship with him by giving him time and walking in the light (1 John 1:7), we will go with the Spirit's flow. We will feel it when we are displeasing him. We will recognise what he is doing and saying.

I say 'extremely' sensitive. Take medical technology, for example. There are instruments in some hospitals today that are so advanced and sensitive that they may uncover a malady that could not have been detected, only twenty years ago. How much more should our own anointing increase so that we are much, much more sensitive to the Spirit's ways than we would have been years ago. I simply want to miss nothing God is in; this is why I would hopefully make the case that we be extremely sensitive to the Spirit. The Spirit is easily grieved. Only a high level of sensitivity to the Spirit will recognise the Spirit elsewhere: in the word that is preached, in the prophetic word, in various manifestations.

How *can* we become open if we fear we are not open but want to be open?

- Be sure there is no unconfessed sin in your life (1 John 1:9).

- Be sure there is no bitterness or grudge against anyone (Eph. 4:31ff.).

- Be sure you do not speak against anyone (James 3).

- Be sure you have a solid prayer and Bible reading life (Luke 18:1; 2 Tim. 2:15).

- Walk in all the light God gives you (1 John 1:7).

- Learn to know the Spirit's voice (Heb. 3:7–8).

- Develop a familiarity with his ways and the ability to recognise his presence (Heb. 3:10–11).

Do not assume you are open to the Spirit today just because you may have been yesterday. I know the feeling of having gone through a hard time, all because I had been open to the Spirit, and saying to myself afterwards, 'I'm not going through anything like that again.' That is the way I felt after I survived the trouble that followed Arthur Blessitt's visit. But God would let me have no such luxury for long.

Do not assume you are open because you have taken a strong stand on some valid issue. For example, you can take a stand on specific issues such as abortion, inspiration of scripture or sound teaching, and not be necessarily open to the Spirit. You could even have the gifts of the Spirit and not be open; after all, they are irrevocable (Rom. 11:29).

Do not assume you are open to the Spirit because God is blessing you. You may be prospering. You may have been healed. You may have a good job. You may know God's guidance.

The consequence of not being open is horrendous; it could mean that you cannot enter God's rest (Heb. 3:7–11). Or that God has sworn an oath against you (Heb. 3:11). It could mean you cannot hear him speak again (Heb. 5:11ff.) or that you cannot be renewed again to repentance (Heb. 6:6).

But if we are open to the Spirit – and able to recognise him at work, we will be at peace with ourselves. We are not likely to miss what he is doing.

Tomorrow's Anointing

The Lord has sought out a man after his own heart. (1 Sam. 13:14)

After removing Saul, he made David their king. He testified concerning him: 'I have found David son of Jesse a man after my own heart; he will do everything I want him to do.' (Acts 13:22)

Saul became yesterday's man because he did not keep the Lord's command. 'I thought, "Now the Philistines will come down against me at Gilgal, and I have not sought the LORD's favour." So I felt compelled to offer the burnt offering' (1 Sam. 13:12). Yesterday's man or woman always has their own excuse why they didn't obey. God found a man after his own heart – David – who would keep the Lord's command. Once he had been anointed by Samuel the Spirit of the Lord came upon David in power 'from that day on' (1 Sam. 16:13).

There are two things, therefore, that would characterise David's anointing: the simultaneous combination of the word (the Lord's command) and the Spirit (power). If you had to determine which of these two ingredients was weightier with David – that is, which would mostly explain his success – you would be hard pressed. It would be almost impossible to tell. The word *and* the Spirit lay behind all that David did. It was the combination that made the difference.

How do you explain the Psalms with their emphasis on the word? It goes back to the Spirit coming on David in power. How do you explain his miraculous escape from Saul, his conquering Jerusalem, his repeated victories over the Philistines? It is traceable to his keeping the Lord's command. For David the two were inseparable and it is impossible to tell which was more important to him.

The high-water mark of David's kingship was when he brought the ark of the Covenant to Jerusalem. 'David, wearing a linen ephod, danced before the LORD with all his might' (2 Sam. 6:14).

The ark represented the word and the Spirit. In it were the tablets of stone (the Ten Commandments, representing the word) together with Aaron's staff that had budded and the jar of manna (representing the miraculous, or power of the Spirit). The ark symbolised the glory of God in ancient Israel. For when the ark had been captured it was said: 'The glory has departed from Israel' (1 Sam. 4:21).

The ark, then, was the symbol of the *kabodh* – the glory of God.[1] The Hebrew *kabodh* also means 'weightiness', and best depicts God's weight, or stature. We sometimes refer to one who 'throws his weight around'. That's the idea – weightiness. God's glory is weighty and powerful. It was the glory that mirrored the combination of the word and Spirit. And David decided it was time to bring the ark to Jerusalem. It had been in a remote spot in Judah since the days of Saul. No one had enquired of it since the days of Saul (1 Chron. 13:3).

David's idea of bringing the ark to Jerusalem was a noble if not lofty plan, but it initially failed. It had not crossed David's mind that bringing the ark to Jerusalem would be difficult. It was merely a matter of transporting it some twenty miles. But it failed. They set the ark on a cart, carried along by oxen. A man called Uzzah reached out and took hold of the ark because the oxen stumbled. 'The LORD's anger burned against

Uzzah because of his irreverent act; therefore God struck him down and he died there beside the ark of God' (2 Sam. 6:7).

We may think that bringing the glory of God to its rightful place in the Church is an easy matter – as easy as David thought it would be to have oxen carry the ark twenty miles to Jerusalem. I wish it were easy! It is not.

David was upset. It was his first failure. The man who killed Goliath, who led Israel in one battle after another in defeating the Philistines and who did the unthinkable – conquering Jerusalem – could not get a small oblong chest twenty miles!

David's emotions went through two stages: from anger to fear. His initial reaction to Uzzah's death was anger with God because of 'the LORD's wrath' (2 Sam. 6:8). But he calmed down and became 'afraid of the LORD that day' (2 Sam. 6:9).

To restore the honour of God's name to the Church is no small enterprise. We may be highly successful in all else we do – organising missions and conferences, preparing good sermons, writing books, writing hymns, getting big crowds and obtaining a bit of a profile. But to see the glory return to the Church is not so easy. David thought it would be a walk-over, a piece of cake. Wrong.

The greatest achievement that the modern Church could possibly witness would be the restoration of God's glory. There is no greater goal, an aim than which no greater can be conceived. It would come, I believe, by bringing the word and the Spirit together – in emphasis and experience. But this isn't as simple as it may seem.

The sudden death of Uzzah over his trying to steady the ark got David's attention. I sometimes wonder what will get our attention. How concerned are we to see the glory of the Lord in the Church? Or is it our own glory and sense of pride that motivates us?

David, however, found what had gone wrong. His perspective had overlooked what God had prescribed about the ark in his word. 'It was because you, the Levites, did not bring

it up the first time that the Lord our God broke out in anger
against us. We did not enquire of him about how to do it in
the prescribed way' (1 Chron. 15:13). *The prescribed way* was
that the Levites alone were to carry the ark with poles on
their shoulders; even *they* could never physically touch it.

David had neglected the explicit prescription that showed
how to regard the ark – the symbol of the glory of the Lord.
God's integrity was on the line; his word was at stake. His
word is magnified above all his name (Ps. 138:2 AV). Had
God allowed David to transport the ark in a manner contrary
to God's word, the eventual result would have been no regard
for that word at all. God wouldn't bend the rules for David –
or you and me.

Nothing has changed. God has set a priority on his word.
God is jealous for his glory. He does not show favouritism.
His word must matter to us or we too *will* fail.

David eventually succeeded in getting the ark to Jerusalem.
It was the happiest day of his life. I'm not sure how much he
would have appreciated his accomplishment had the attempt
not failed the first time.

If the word and the Spirit come together in the Church –
both in emphasis and in experience – it will be the happiest
event in many years.

David's achievement and anointing would show the result
of the simultaneous and inseparable combination of the word
and the Spirit. It was Israel's greatest era; David was Israel's
greatest king. David was a man after God's own heart.

God's own heart is that the word and Spirit should be
equally recognised in emphasis. It can be easily argued that
the two are always inseparable – for this is absolutely true. For
it is by the Spirit that we receive the word; it is the word that
tells us about the Spirit. *They cannot be separated.*

And yet saying that is not the total picture. Jesus said to his
disciples, 'You are already clean because of the word I have
spoken to you' (John 15:3), yet Jesus later breathed on them

and said, 'Receive the Holy Spirit' (John 20:22). This shows that there was more that they needed, even though they had the word. Jesus said to the Father, 'I gave them the words you gave me and they accepted them' (John 17:8) and yet he later told them to stay in Jerusalem 'until you have been clothed with power from on high' (Luke 24:49). Jesus himself was the Word made flesh but he too received the Spirit (Luke 3:22; John 1:33ff.). Therefore when we say that the word and the Spirit are inseparable we need to state what we mean. For it is possible that one may have the full and undiluted word but have the Spirit in less measure. That was the disciples' experience prior to Pentecost.

My own experience across the years has been largely to emphasise the word. But that does not mean I don't have a measure of the Spirit. I could not have preached the word with some power without the Spirit. As for those who emphasise the Spirit – signs, wonders, gifts of the Spirit – they are not devoid of the word. Without the word they would not even know about such things as gifts of the Spirit. We are therefore talking about the degree, or measure, one has of either the word or the Spirit in one's own ministry.

So they can be separated in *emphasis*. And if they are separated by *emphasising* one over the other it should not be surprising that there will be corresponding results. These results are seen in what amounts to a cleavage in the modern Church. I call it a silent divorce between the word and the Spirit. It is not what God has done but what man has done. Some have chosen to stress the word to the neglect of an equal stress on the Spirit.

The problem is, those who stress preaching the word sometimes say that by merely emphasising the word you automatically *get the Holy Spirit thrown in*, as it were, since the word and the Spirit cannot be separated. Those who emphasise the Holy Spirit say that by doing so you are but being *true to the word*! I have found, generally speaking, that neither side sees a neglect on their part. Each sincerely believes that they are correct in their emphasis and balanced in their understanding.

I see both sides. I have been on both sides. I have been closely involved with those on both sides. I know how each feels and thinks – dare I say it – backwards and forwards.

The truth is, some *are* more open to the word than others; some are more open to the Spirit than others. To get those who are (in my opinion) less open to the word to *admit* that is like pushing a car uphill with your little finger. And to get those who are (in my opinion) less open to the Spirit to *admit* such is like holding on to the back bumper of a car with your little finger as that car takes off.

The impasse is enormous. Who will become vulnerable and admit to a neglect? Are we not all like those in the church of Laodicea who say that they are rich and have need of nothing (Rev. 3:17)? The truth is, we are neither hot nor cold – we are lukewarm and of little use. This includes those of us who are strong on the word but are scared to death of manifestations of the Spirit and stay suspicious of the miraculous. This includes those who are strong on manifestations of the Spirit but are impatient with theology and too often take the Gospel for granted. No one pleads guilty.

I said some of these things to a group of three hundred ministers in Toronto when I was kindly invited by John Arnott to preach at the Airport Christian Fellowship. I took questions at the end and one minister asked: 'Who do you think are more open – the word people being open to the Spirit or the Spirit people being open to the word?' My answer was that *initially* the people on the Spirit side seem more open but at the end of the day it is about fifty-fifty.

Those generally seen as open to the Spirit are usually those who are at home with the gifts of the Spirit. And their openness shows – they have a freedom and love for the Lord that is sometimes very uninhibited. I think it is wonderful.

The word people tend to be more uptight – fearful of showing emotions, and sometimes seemingly afraid to smile!

The Spirit people, then, *seem* more open. That is, initially. But if you suggested to some of them that they might not be all that open to the word *they* can get very uptight and defensive.

I will never forget a conversation I had with some major Christian leaders, when I was trying to make the case that so many so-called Spirit-filled Christians are bored with preaching and serious Bible study. 'I resent that,' said one. I then pointed out how Paul Cain had brought in the emphasis on holiness to a large group of so-called Spirit-filled Christians. In the beginning the leaders were excited and open, but in the end they backed off. I thought this was quite sad. But my friends defended those leaders: 'They would have lost 80 per cent of their people had they kept on emphasising holiness.' Really? That was precisely my point! If 80 per cent were not open to the emphasis on holiness, whatever is that but an emphasis on the word? That conversation to me was a dead give-away that too many Christians are open to the Spirit but are not very open to the word!

We are not talking about dishonest people. Those representing both sides are godly and sincere. If you put them under a lie detector you would see that they are telling the truth. The word people can detect heresy a mile away. The Spirit people can smell dead orthodoxy a mile away.

Tomorrow's anointing will close the gap. 'Give ear and come to me; hear me, that your soul may live. I will make an everlasting covenant with you, my faithful love promised to David' (Isa. 55:3). When we learn to forgive one another totally and come to see our pitiful bankruptcy, we will be getting close to tomorrow's anointing. When we cease attacking one another and worry about the Philistines outside the family rather than competing with one another, we will be getting close.

It will be recalled that Saul became more obsessed with David than he was with the Philistines, whom he should have been more worried about. It is told that when President Richard Nixon welcomed the first astronaut who walked on the moon, when Neil Armstrong returned to earth in the South Pacific, Nixon himself was actually more interested in what had just happened in Chappaquidick – an event that sealed Senator Edward Kennedy's political destiny. Ted Kennedy could have run for president had not his friend Mary Jo Kopechne drowned on that awful night. Kennedy – Nixon's political rival – had Nixon's attention more than Neil Armstrong, who made world history. As for King Saul, he lost his life in the end because he *hadn't* succeeded in keeping the Philistines at bay. By concentrating on David he lost everything.

We need to close ranks and become vulnerable. We need to see the enemy – the devil – who is at ease as long as we defend our own party line rather than be devoted to truth, whichever side it is coming from.

During the first week I met Paul Cain we discussed John Wimber's comment that he blamed himself for David Watson's death. Sensing that Paul identified with Wimber I said, 'Paul, you need my theology – I need your power.' He replied, 'Help me.' We made a covenant to be open to each other and be mutually open to the word and the Spirit; it was in that moment that our hope for the word and Spirit to come together was born. Not that this had not been recognised before but I suspect this conviction was given a fresh impetus at that time. We both began to feel we had a destiny together. Paul seemed to represent openness to the Spirit; I came from a reformed perspective that is almost entirely word-centred.

It was at the aforementioned Word and Spirit conference at Wembley that I first preached on Matthew 22:29: 'Jesus replied, "You are in error because you do not know the Scriptures or the power of God." ' The Sadducees, said Jesus, were ignorant of both. It is my observation that most of today's Church, speaking generally, emphasises either one or the other.

I had a meal with John Wimber three years ago at his hotel near Holy Trinity Brompton. That very morning God gave me a word for John Wimber. I began to dread my time with this highly esteemed servant of Christ. But during the meal I turned to him and said, 'John, God has given me a word for you.' He was eager to hear it.

I began by saying, 'I agreed with every word I heard you say at Royal Albert Hall the other night.'

'Really?' he responded with a clear tone of appreciation.

I reminded him of what he said: 'Luther and Calvin gave us the *word* in the sixteenth century, but God wants us to see his *works* in the twentieth century.' John agreed that is what he said.

'But John,' I continued, 'you are teaching Pharaohs who knew not Joseph' – that is the word I felt God gave me for John Wimber. The Pharaoh who had honoured Joseph died and the new generation of Israel was under a Pharaoh who knew nothing about Joseph. 'John, you are assuming that these people who are required to do the *works* have the *word*, just because that came in the sixteenth century. John, people today don't even know the *word*.'

He put his knife and fork down, looking me in the eye, 'You have put your finger on the very vortex' – pointing to his heart – 'of my thinking at this moment. I accept what you have said.' He promised to take that word on board.

Whether he began to apply my word to him after that, I do not know. I do know he humbly accepted what I said and said he agreed with me. I have always appreciated him for that.

Take those of us, if I may say it one more time, who represent the word tradition. We say: the need of the hour is preaching, getting back to the faith once delivered to the saints. We must recover our reformation heritage, stress the doctrines of justification by faith, the sovereignty of God, assurance of salvation. We need to recover the emphasis of Edwards, Whitefield and Spurgeon. People today do not know their Bibles, they do not know theology. We must get back to the word.

Take those who represent the Spirit tradition. They say: the need of the hour is for signs and wonders, the gifts of the Holy Spirit to be in operation. We need those with prophetic gifts, gifts of healing so that the world will see there is a God of wonders who is alive and well. What is needed is for the power of God to be displayed as it was in the book of Acts, when the place was literally shaken.

What is wrong with either emphasis? I answer: nothing. Each is exactly right. But neither is complete. It is not one or the other that is needed, it is both. What is needed, in my opinion, is a re-marriage of the word and the Spirit. But I do not mean by that a sort of ecumenical coming together of churches (however desirable that may be). What is needed is the simultaneous combination of both the word and the Spirit in today's servant of Christ and the Church. It seems that one or the other is present in most cases – but usually not both.

I repeat: you cannot separate the two. The presence of the word presupposes the Spirit as well. For example, any converted person became a Christian *because* of the word preached (Rom. 10:8) and that could not be received without the Holy Spirit. No one can say Jesus is Lord but by the Holy Spirit (1 Cor. 12:3). So where the word is, the Spirit is. But one can emphasise one or the other less and the result will be less of each in our experience.

When Paul said, 'Our gospel came to you not simply with words, but also with power, with the Holy Spirit' (1 Thess. 1:5), he was admitting to the possibility of that preaching coming without power. Every preacher (if honest) knows what it is like to preach without power. Paul's preaching at Thessalonica was with power. That is how he knew they were converted (1 Thess. 1:4). But it follows that one could say all the right things, be totally sound theologically and be of no effect. 'Perfectly orthodox, perfectly useless,' Dr Lloyd-Jones used to say. It is not that the word and Spirit are divided to the extent that there is all word and no Spirit or all Spirit and no word; the charge is the lack of balance of the two together, and this is what I am calling for.

The problem is, you can't get many people on either side to see much deficiency! Again, take those who are on the word side of the spectrum: 'We do have the Spirit,' they say with hand on heart. They really do mean that. It is largely to people like that that one has to press an idea of openness to the Spirit. 'But I am open,' such a person would say. Take those who are on the Spirit side of the equation: 'We do have the word,' they will tell you – and sincerely believe that. You would offend such people if you suggested that they are not all that open to the word. We are therefore at an impasse.

One has to say that, for the most part, the current move of the Spirit that has stressed manifestations of the Spirit has not issued in many conversions. I thank God for the exceptions, and I am aware that there are happy exceptions. But by and large the world generally is not awakened.

I pray that this will change – soon. When people come to hear me preach they don't really expect to see anything, they expect to hear. 'Thank you for your word,' they might say. That's what they expected and that's what they got. I suppose there are places where people go largely to see – to observe the miraculous and the manifestations. But if the word and the Spirit come together in your anointing and mine, then, as my dear friend Lyndon Bowring said, 'Those who come to see will hear, and those who come to hear will see.' That is tomorrow's anointing and when it comes the world will be awakened.

I pray that the anointing of Almighty God will rest on you.

Notes

Chapter 1: The Anointing

1   Chrism oil is also used to anoint Roman Catholics at baptism, confirmation and ordination, as well as at many other church ceremonies.
2   We now make this available after our evening services. Those who request the anointing of oil do so by sitting in a designated area.
3   However, there were times when a prophet too was directly anointed. The Lord told Elijah to anoint Jehu (1 Kgs. 19:16).

Chapter 2: Accepting our Anointing

1   R T Kendall, *God Meant it for Good* (Paternoster 1998).

Chapter 11: The Secret Anointing

1   However, there is another story regarding Spurgeon's rejection by Regent's Park College. At the interview for the college, it is said, the principal was in one room waiting for Spurgeon while Spurgeon was in another room waiting for the principal. They remained there for an hour or

so waiting for each other. By the time the error was discovered the principal had given up and gone home.
Spurgeon reckoned the incident was providential and
made no further attempt to apply to Regent's.

Chapter 12: The Anointing

1   By 'return' I do not mean restoration of salvation. Griev-
    ing the Holy Spirit does not forfeit salvation. After all, the
    Spirit seals us for the day of redemption (Eph. 4:30). What
    we forfeit is not our salvation but presence of mind –
    clear thinking. When the dove returns it means a return
    of clear thinking and sense of his presence.

Chapter 13: Openness to God's Word

1   This is a literal translation of the Hebrew which most
    modern versions sadly overlook. Only the Living Bible
    has a footnote in which it says that the literal translation
    is: 'You have magnified your word above all your name.'
2   Wayne Grudem, *Systematic Theology* (Zondervan 1994),
    pp. 47–140.
3   God's secret will also pertains to his purpose for us from
    all eternity.

Chapter 14: Openness to the Holy Spirit

1   Psalm 51 is the prayer of David the returning backslider
    after he was confronted by Nathan the prophet (2 Sam.
    12:1–14).
2   This phrase was taught to me by Dr Lloyd-Jones. I first
    recall hearing it from his lips many years ago when he
    preached for me at my Southern Baptist Church in Lower
    Heyford. I had just written a catechism for our young
    people and put in the question: 'How do you know the

Bible is the word of God?' Answer: 'By the witness of the Holy Spirit.' When I showed this catechism to Dr Lloyd-Jones he urged me to put the answer: 'By the *immediate and direct* witness of the Holy Spirit.' This matter was of crucial importance to him and has shaped my own thinking profoundly.

Chapter 15: Tomorrow's Anointing

1   The Hebrew word *kabodh* refers to the visible or detachable radiation of God's character. It is linked with ideas of honour, brilliance, distinction.

Scripture Index

The Anointing

8:7	122	18:8–9	80
10:1	15	18:9	75, 145
10:6	16	18:10–11	81
10:9	16, 60	18:12	81
10:9–11	52	18:14	156
10:10–11	16	18:25	82
10:11	60	18:29	151
11:6–8	63	19:6	82
13:8–9	38, 63	19:9–10	83
13:9–14	38	19:11–23	81
13:11	64	19:23	12
13:11–12	64	19:24	61
13:12	193	20:18–42	145
13:13–14	38, 64	23:7–29	81
13:14	139, 193	24:4	159
15:1	76	24:5	159
15:1–3	64	24:6	13, 15, 60
15:3	79	24:6–7	160
15:22–3	65	24:16–17	148
16:1	ix, 12, 15, 16, 59 (2), 63,	25:12–34	162
	99, 110, 122, 126, 127	25:32–4	162
16:2	110	26:8	161
16:6	128	26:9	60, 161
16:7	128, 153	26:10–11	162
16:9	128	26:21	66
16:10	128	28:7ff.	83
16:11	129, 130, 153, 155	28:15	66, 78
16:11–12	120, 130		
16:12	120, 131	2 Samuel	
16:13	16, 60, 139, 147, 163,	2:4	163 (2)
	177, 193	6:7	195
16:14	12, 16, 74	6:8	195
16:18	140	6:9	195
16:23	75, 140	6:14	194
17:8–11	142	12	67
17:25	142	12:1–14	205
17:26	142	12:11–12	67
17:28	155	12:13	67
17:29	155	13—24	68
17:32	142	23:1	140
17:33	142		
17:34–7	143	1 Kings	
17:39	143	17:7	111
17:40	144	18:21	17
17:42–7	144	18:36	17
17:49	144	18:39	17
17:50	144	19:16	204
18:2–3	145	21:21–2	76
18:7	75, 80, 147	21:27	77
18:8	145	21:28–9	77

Scripture Index

Scripture Index

2 Corinthians
2:16	111
3:12	118
3:17	40
3:18	78
4:4–5	176
5:10	19, 34, 56, 134
10:10	35, 129
10:13	25, 32
11:6	35
11:14	115
11:23–5	88

Galatians
3:8	165
5:11	88
5:22	27, 119
5:22ff.	172
6:1	79
6:17	87

Ephesians
1:3	185
1:11	179
2:1–8	176
4:30	12, 50, 157, 190, 205
4:30ff.	190
4:31ff.	191
4:31–2	50, 159
5:18	185

Philippians
1:12	132

1 Thessalonians
1:4	202
1:5	202
4:3–7	117
5:19	12, 190
5:20	174

2 Thessalonians
2:11	83

1 Timothy
5:18	174

2 Timothy
1:7	190
2:15	191

3:16	117, 173

Hebrews
1:14	22
2:10	147
3:7–8	191
3:7–11	77, 188, 192
3:10–11	191
3:11	192
4:16	119
5:8	147
5:11	77, 121, 186
5:11ff.	192
6:4–6	78, 79 (4)
6:6	192
6:10	134
9:14	17
11	95, 133, 187 (3)
11:2	17
11:4	65
11:5	96
11:7	96
11:8	96
11:39–40	134
12:6	27, 66
13:7	91
13:8	91

James
1:5	13
1:17	23
3	191
4:6	118
5:14	14
5:14–15	16

1 Peter
1:12	134
2:15	156
3:13	118
3:13–14	156
5:7	49
5:8	115

2 Peter
1:21	117, 174
3:16	174

1 John
1:7	24, 78, 190, 191